Guidance
24/7

How to Open Your Heart

and Live Intuitively with

Divine Direction

Christel Nani, RN, Medical Intuitive

Queen's Court Press
Phoenix, AZ

Library of Congress Cataloguing-in-Publication Data
Nani, Christel
Guidance 24/7: how to open your heart and
live intuitively with divine direction /
Christel Nani. – 2nd ed.
p. cm.
Alternative healing. 2. Spirituality. 3. Intuition.
Library of Congress Control Number: 2009924023

ISBN: 9780974145082

Printed in the United States of America
Second Edition

To my Mom & Dad
for teaching me the importance of integrity,
forgiveness, and compassion, and for making me
the person I am today.

My profound gratitude
to God, St. Jude, and all the angels,
for your unwavering help and support.

For all of my clients
who are smart and courageous
and have learned to ask for help!

Also by Christel Nani

BOOKS

DIARY OF A MEDICAL INTUITIVE: *One Woman's Eye-Opening Journey from No-Nonsense E.R. Nurse to Open-Hearted Healer and Visionary*
SACRED CHOICES: *Thinking Outside the Tribe to Heal Your Spirit (Random House)*

CDs

Healing Your First Three Chakras
The Confidence Code: *A Guide to Building Self-Esteem and Living Courageously*
Transforming Your Archetypes: *Healing the Big Four within You: Child-Victim-Saboteur-Prostitute*

CHRISTEL CARDS

Prayers to Raise Your Vibration

Christel Nani

CONTENTS

Foreword to the 2nd Edition of *Guidance 24/7*

Welcome to the second edition of *Guidance 24/7*! Christel has written a fantastic guide to the spiritual life. If you follow her instructions, you'll be up and running with your guidance and intuition in no time. In fact, this is the hallmark of Christel's work: creating a high vibration life in no time!

What I love most about Christel's work is that it is direct, practical and effective. There's no woo-woo, no weird hierarchy of rituals or certifications; there is simply the truth: Divine help is available to all and you can easily start receiving guidance to make your life better.

I know this because I have taught with Christel for many years now, following my own healing from multiple sclerosis. You don't need an intermediary, nor travel to a foreign country to have enlightenment. The path is easy and direct, *if*, and this is a big one, *if you're willing to be spiritually responsible.*

Being spiritually responsible means stepping up to the plate, looking at the results of your life choices, and learning to make different and higher vibration decisions to be happier and healthier, bringing the world to what Christel calls "the tipping point of positivity."

If you are ready to tap into your intuition, do it with integrity. You can't ask with insincerity, or worse, with victim energy, with an intention to fail and then blame the failure on God. You can't get away with that stuff on the path to spiritual responsibility.

Christel teaches quite simply: ask for guidance with a sincere heart and you will hear an answer. Follow that guidance and your life will improve immeasurably. There are many instances of people healing in our retreats and workshops when they realized how to stop their energy drains and quickly and genuinely raise their vibration, by tapping into intuition.

Guidance 24/7 can help you do it too.

Rebecca Grace, Psy.D.

March, 2009

Chapter One

HOW INTUITIVE ARE YOU?

You have a sixth sense, a spiritual ability, and a profound gift at your fingertips any time you need it. Called intuition, guidance, or inner knowing, it is your birthright and available to you at all times.

You can learn how to use it to protect you, help you answer questions, solve problems, and give you peace of mind when life gets bumpy, and you can learn to tap into it whenever you want.

My experiences as a clairvoyant have taught me that you are more intuitive than you realize. I also know that intuition needs to be honed and used daily to develop fully. With the right tools, you can learn to hear your intuition, receive spiritual messages and communicate with your soul, the source of your inner wisdom.

This wisdom, a mother's intuition, a hunch, gut feeling, persistent urging, a premonition, or an instinctual inner knowing, tells you when your friend needs a call, or gives you a feeling not to drive on a particular road. Detectives and doctors often follow a hunch that help them solve a case or make a diagnosis.

My inner knowing is a gift passed down to me, not only from my mother, but my grandmothers and great-grandmothers on both sides of my family. Living in such a household was rather interesting; my mother with her own profound intuitive gift, always knew who instigated a noisy event, or was the catalyst for a broken lamp among my siblings, without any evidence to back her up. She just knew.

This insight may be helpful with a house full of children but can also help you live an easier life. Intuition or guidance is knowledge relayed to you from outside of your cognitive world; it comes from your spirit, the smart part of you that is most like what people call God or Higher Power.

Your spirit communicates from a neutral place and sees with a divine perspective providing more solutions than you would normally see. Isn't it wonderful to know that you don't have to work so hard to figure things out? And that it's free for the asking!

Intention controls your intuition

Intuition responds very sensitively to your intentions. If your intention is undecided or ambivalent, your intuitive messages will be fuzzy and vague. If you decide to shut your intuition out, it will go silent. And if you decide you want true help and guidance, it will respond with immediate direction that you will understand.

The best way to start is to simply ask for what you need such as guidance, help, answers, the next step, or confirmation on what you may have already decided to do. If you have trouble quieting your mind or your head is filled with chatter, use one of the techniques below, but remember to direct your request to a high vibration source such as God or Higher Power.

Here are some simple techniques to begin:

- Set an intention when you go to sleep to have a dream that shows you the answer to your conundrum. "I want to have a clear dream that gives me an answer to my question."

- Program your mind before you fall asleep to awaken with the knowledge of the secret hiding place of your lost glasses or keys: "I'd like to wake up and know where I can find my glasses."

- Say a prayer (a form of focused communication) to God, Higher Power, or your spiritual helpers. The prayer can be as simple as a single word: "help."

- Sit quietly and focus on your question, and open your heart to receiving an answer. Repeating an energetic intention such as, "I am excited to receive intuitive guidance that will show me what to do about _____," will work.

- Ask for a sign that you are moving in the right direction.

- Visualize yourself in the future telling friends how clear your guidance was and how much more you are hearing and following your intuition. Imagine telling them the benefits of following your inner instructions.

Things that will not help are saying affirmations such as, "I am open to all that the universe will provide for me," or "I am ready to follow my guidance when I receive it." The first is unfocused and terribly nebulous and the second takes you a step beyond listening to action that you may not be ready for.

Sincere asking is the key to getting real answers. Part of being sincere in asking for guidance is not putting conditions on the answer. It doesn't work to pray, "Dear God, show me what to do but don't make it be X or Y." I remember being plagued by some painful physical symptoms and going for tests to determine their cause.

I had already done an intuitive scan of myself and I knew what the diagnosis was, but I hadn't liked what I learned. I was hoping for a different answer. The lab ran my tests several times; sometimes they came back positive, sometimes negative. My doctors were baffled. I kept praying for a diagnosis but heard nothing. *This is strange,* I thought. *I have never been without an answer to prayer.*

More weeks of praying and still there was silence. Finally, I looked within myself to see if my prayer was sincere. I had to face the fact that because I was ignoring the diagnosis God showed me in the first place, my prayer for a diagnosis wasn't sincere.

I already knew the answer but wanted a different "truth." I decided that I truly did want to know what was wrong with me, and that night I prayed differently. I surrendered to God's will, acknowledged my fear of hearing the truth, and trusted that God would be there for me. In other words, I took away the conditions I had set on the guidance I was asking for.

Within a very short time, the lab was able to confirm the diagnosis of what was wrong; it was the same answer I had been given intuitively. However, I had to genuinely want the answer, not just say I wanted it.

When you pray for guidance, you cannot attach conditions or rules such as *tell me this but not that.* If you're worried that the answer you're going to get is not one you're going to like, your intention will not be clear, focused, strong, or integrious, which sends a message to your spirit to block your intuition.

Trying to control or impose conditions on your spiritual information will also disconnect you as Fran was from her spirit. On the surface Fran's request sounds like she was asking for guidance, but listen to what she is really saying:

"Dear God,

I have a problem in my relationship; I'm not happy and my spouse isn't going to change. I don't know what to do, but it feels like my life is slowly draining out of me. I'm often tired, not fully happy, and need to disconnect from my significant other on a routine basis to avoid feeling so badly. I need some guidance and help on my next step.

P.S. Please don't tell me to end my relationship because I'm not willing, I can't do it, and because we've been together for twelve years, and I'm too old to start over. Amen."

Fran knew her relationship was toxic and that she needed to leave. She wasn't really asking for an answer. Her request won't be answered because she is not sincere. If you are not ready to hear an answer, just pray for comfort, courage, and trust until you are ready.

Hearing your intuitive hunches is dependent upon you wanting to hear them. Ask clearly and you will receive a clear answer. However, as Fran learned, you have to really want it.

Your logical mind or your heart cannot confine your intuition. Intuition does not guide you based upon worldly rules, weighing the pros and cons of each situation. Spiritual information is succinct and brief (there is no dissertation involved). You hear, "forgive yourself, sell your business, rest, or stop everything." A quiet voice at first, it comes from a place beyond judgment, fear, distraction, or what appears to be logic. There is no emotion attached to it.

When you are in touch with your intuition, you are in a place of profound power from being in alignment with your spirit and in communication with the divine.

Intuition and inspiration

You know that intuition is a sudden knowing that comes without logic, thought, or effort. It is when you simply know something is true or right. An inspiration, on the other hand, is a revelation, an idea that's quite outside of your normal way of thinking. It is creative – it pulls you up and out of your old ways. Inspiration is also a gift from the divine – think of Michelangelo, Beethoven, or the moment you realized that your life didn't have to be as hard as you were making it.

Inspiration stimulates your creativity and opens you to seeing surprising solutions to difficult problems. Inspiration motivates and encourages you to be dynamic and open to changes in your life. We can't take all the credit for those bright ideas that seem to just pop into our heads one morning. Remember to say thank you!

Paying attention to your inspiration and listening to your intuition will raise your vibration, as your spirit provides you with the necessary information to evolve to an easier and more joyous life.

Although this divine information is available 24/7 and will guide you to a better place, you may not trust it because you aren't clear if it is real or just your own thoughts. Remember that inspiration comes from outside your normal thinking, while intuition is usually more subtle, leaving you to wonder if you imagined the information. But there are very clear differences between intuitive whispers and the chatter of your mind.

Once you understand these differences, it will be so much easier to trust your intuitive knowing. There are two important qualities that are hallmarks of both intuition and inspiration:

- *The information is brief.* "Fire your doctor, stay away from your abusive friend, build houses for Habitat for Humanity, adopt a child, go to France, create a pet rock, take a road trip, or spend time with your family now because you are dying soon."

- *There is no emotional component.* The information is neutral, clear, and free from fear, doubt, anxiety, or any other emotion.

Divine instruction is never obsessive, is always the best action for you, and speaks briefly and then is quiet. It is unambiguous, simple, and direct, often coming in seven words or less. Your intuition won't be vague; you'll know what you are supposed to do.

Your thoughts, however, will go round and round throughout the night with with no resolution, creating fearful scenarios, draining your energy and leaving you exhausted and conflicted. When your mind is churning, it's not divine information. Now think back to the peace of an intuitive hit, and experience the contrast.

One of the most important things you can do, is to train yourself to know your brand of intuition. What does it sound like, look like, and feel like? Is it a voice in your head, skywriting across your mind, a peaceful feeling, or a comforting warmth that says this is true?

Keep track of your intuitive hits in a journal to become aware of your particular intuitive style. Note the words you heard, the picture you saw, or the thought that popped into your head.

Listening to divine information keeps you young and vibrant.

Should you trust that voice in your head?

Once you get the hang of your intuitive expression, your confidence in trusting divine information will grow. Whether you hear a quiet voice or an insistent voice, both are worth paying attention to. Rebecca learned this in two back-to-back powerful experiences:

"While in graduate school, I was studying at my desk when I suddenly heard a clear voice urgently commanding me to *move now*. I pushed back my chair and took a step away from my desk when without warning, the heavy textbooks and the shelves above me collapsed onto my chair. Had I not moved when my inner voice told me to, I could have easily suffered a head injury or worse.

Shortly thereafter I was driving during a heavy rainstorm on a high-speed freeway that winds around downtown Seattle. This section is notoriously dangerous as the road narrows, heavy overpasses crisscross the freeway, and traffic does not slow down. I turned on my blinker to change lanes and as I began to turn my steering wheel, I heard a soft *wait*. I turned the wheel a fraction of an inch before it locked, and although it jammed I felt strangely calm even though I was in heavy rush hour traffic.

In the next instant, a small convertible sped by me from my blind spot, even harder to see because of the car's tiny size and the heavy rain. Had I made my lane change, I would have run right in to him and been the catalyst of a high speed accident involving many cars.

In a fraction of a second, the sports car had cleared my space and my steering returned to normal. I know that divine intervention spared more than two lives that day."

Whether you hear gentle whispers
or booming commands,
your guidance will come
in a way that is divinely ordained for you.

One afternoon two people who consider themselves healers were visiting a friend, Alice. After a brief visit, Alice said she was tired and needed to lie down. Her two friends offered to do some healing work on her.

The two friends became very focused on their work and neglected to notice the change in Alice. She developed indigestion and said she felt cold. Her friends noticed her skin became clammy and intensified their efforts.

Pale, tired, and unwell, Alice quietly endured their ministrations until finally she felt too sick to continue. She told her well-meaning friends that she needed to rest. They decided to take a walk around her home and return in about fifteen minutes.

Twice while walking, one of the friends *heard* a voice in her head that said, "go back to Alice." Involved in conversation, she discounted the voice and continued her walk, thinking it was just her anxiety over her friend's illness.

Both friends were so focused on discussing their healing techniques, that their walk took more than the expected fifteen minutes. They returned to the silent house assuming that Alice was either resting or sleeping. When they looked in on her, they found her dead in her bed.

Alice had been in the throes of a massive myocardial infarction, replete with indigestion, sweating, clammy pale skin, nausea, weakness, and profound fatigue. The two friends were so attentive to using their healing techniques, they missed the obvious signs of her heart attack.

Had Alice's friend listened to the persistent voice in her mind, she would have returned in time to call an ambulance and get Alice to a hospital.

When you get a nagging feeling, a powerful thought in your mind, or an unrelenting urging, please don't ignore it. Your sixth sense is engaged and trying to send you an important message.

When you have to take the time to argue with, discount, explain, or rationalize the voice in your head, it's time to pay attention to it.

Chapter Two

THE 48 HOUR RULE

You've asked for help in solving a problem, and now you wait. Hours, days go by and still you hear nothing. What went wrong? Are your spiritual guides on vacation? Did you exceed your quota of help requests? Is your Higher Power or God busy helping someone else or upset with you?

How long before you hear back? It could literally take seconds, or it could take a bit longer. I have never gone more than 48 hours without an answer – unless I did not really want an answer out of fear that I wouldn't like it.

If you pray for guidance about your job and are afraid to learn you must leave it, can you put your heart and soul into your request for an answer? This heartfelt sincerity is a vital requirement to hearing your guidance. Set your intention to hear guidance, but make an agreement with yourself that you don't need to act immediately if you are just not ready.

This agreement to hear but not act right now will keep you in the game so you don't shut down your spiritual evolution, and will decrease your anxiety and move you forward to learn your next step in life.

Spiritual evolution is not static, but is dynamic and requires change and movement. Hearing your guidance is that first step.

Once you've heard your guidance, the next logical step is to follow it. When I heard the soft, clear voice in my head, telling me to leave my beloved work in the E.R. and use my intuitive gifts full-time, I felt the resonance of truth. There was no thinking involved on my part, no decision to make, no inner debate about should I or shouldn't I do this. I didn't like the message, but it came nonetheless with a feeling of complete knowing and lacking any emotional component.

You will know your guidance is genuine guidance because it will run through you in a way that feels true. Truth always resonates inside you, unless you are not fully present or grounded in your body.

When you feel the resonance of truth run through your body, you have connected with your soul.

Take the time to sit quietly for a few moments each day and let go of worldly distractions. Breathe deeply, relax, and review your day, paying close attention to your dreams, the people you've come in contact with, and to coincidences, which are synchronicity in action.

Don't waste time in debate or coming up with a multitude of excuses why your answer doesn't make sense or isn't the best thing for you. It won't change the guidance. Guidance is truth, and truth cannot be negotiated.

You can't negotiate the truth that harming others is wrong. You can't convince yourself otherwise and remain in alignment with your soul.

In that initial moment of hearing your guidance, a relief, a joy, an excitement runs through your whole being until your darn brain thinks it over, sees how it will change your life, and hollers, "Are you crazy? No way!"

During one of my workshops, a lovely man who was a social worker received guidance that it was time to change careers. Deep down, he felt relieved because he wouldn't have to listen to people's problems any more.

His soul and heart were greatly eased until his brain demanded, "How will you support yourself?" That's when his fear kicked in. And when fear kicks in, your rational mind comes up with every logical, rational, and defensive reason not to follow the guidance you have been given.

You won't always like your guidance even though it is always good for you. Sometimes guidance sucks. It appeared to fly in the face of logic for me to set out in a virtually unknown field doing who knows what and who knows how.

All the folks around me said as much at the time. Actually what they said was more like, "You are nuts, crazy, stupid! If you leave your job, what will you do, how will you do it, and how will you support yourself? What if you can't get another job as good as this one?"

Naturally, I couldn't answer those questions because guidance doesn't usually come with a detailed instruction book. We are generally given the goal or the first step toward that goal, but nothing more, until we take that step. What is demanded of us is radical trust.

Do you remember what I said about there being a feeling of truth when guidance comes? No matter how much I hated the guidance I was given to quit my E.R. nursing job and use my psychic gifts full time, deep inside I could still feel it was the right thing for me to do.

Remember that guidance will never appeal to your brain by saying, "You should do this because..."

Now that you've agreed to hear your guidance, the only relevant question to ask yourself is, "How long will I debate my guidance and make myself miserable?" The social worker in my workshop had lasted almost eight years doing something he didn't like, and he was suffering from an incurable disease because his system had become so drained by his work. Hearing guidance to leave his job freed his soul and put him in alignment with his truth.

Following his guidance is what he is working on now, but simply knowing his truth has brought his soul a sense of peace and freedom. He has stopped doing self-destructive things, takes better care of himself, and has begun to let people get closer to him. He also has started praying daily for himself and others. As to his "incurable" illness, he is healing daily.

Robert, a musician, was also set free by following his guidance. He was a successful rock musician with a band but deep down wanted to play mellow acoustic guitar, and he wanted to play it solo. Of course, acoustic guitar solos are not as "cool" as rock music, so he struggled between wanting to keep his "cool" reputation and wanting to follow his heart's desire. Then his fear kicked in and he started thinking, "You were successful playing rock, so stick to what you know."

How could he leave something he was good at to embark on an unknown course? When I asked him if he was ready for whatever answer he received – whether it be to stick with the rock band or go into the unknown world of acoustic guitar – he wasn't sure if he could take action but he was open to hearing the answer, and prayed for divine guidance.

That night Robert had a dream: he was sitting in a doctor's office waiting when a doctor walked in and said,

"If you continue to play rock music, you will go deaf," then walked out. End of dream. Robert didn't need me to interpret the dream. He gave up his connections to rock and roll and began writing music more suited to solo guitar, allowing his true inner voice to come through and move him in a direction of greater happiness.

So how long should you wait? If you haven't heard an answer within 48 hours, you need to go back and honestly check your prayer or intention. Ask yourself:

- Do you really want a truthful answer? Have you put conditions upon your guidance because you are afraid to hear what you already know deep in your soul?

- Are you sincerely open to what's in your highest good, even if it requires changes in your life?

- Are you willing to let go of what seems like the easier path (the one of avoidance) and instead do what's best for your spirit?

The length of time it takes to hear an answer is not determined by the size, but rather the *quality* of your request. If your spiritual hotline hasn't gotten back to you, it's time to call again with genuine sincerity.

Truth is an idea that "feels right" and is in alignment with your soul.

Your intuition is your truth

What's the secret to following guidance that seems to contradict common sense? What gave Robert the ability to walk away from his past success and status in the world of rock? He felt the ring of truth resonate throughout his body as he relayed his dream. How did the social worker live down the sneers of his colleagues when he told them he was going to change careers and work with computers, which he'd always loved? He remembered how his heart had felt the moment he heard his guidance: deeply relieved and very happy.

Do you believe that following your guidance will always make your life better? How can you be sure? Look back to a moment in your life when you had that deep knowing and you chose to listen to it. Remember what it felt like when that truth ran through your body, and left you with a wonderful feeling that led to peace and calmness.

That calmness can help you make the necessary changes that might scare you. People often remark that they just *knew* what they had to do, bringing them to a state of focused clarity, determination and personal power.

Truth is a compelling force that demands your attention, propelling you to act regardless of what others say to or about you. It is so powerful that ignoring it by procrastinating or pretending it isn't true will derail your spiritual growth, keep you stuck, and maybe even create physical symptoms.

Your truth, unfortunately, is sometimes the last thing you want to hear, because it often requires changes in your neatly packaged, *looks good from the outside* life.

My life changed dramatically after listening to the completely illogical guidance to leave my beloved job in the E.R. And guess what? Even though my life was good then, it's a thousand times better now on all levels, and yours will be too, if you don't negotiate your truth.

- Negotiating doesn't change the correct course of action for you; it merely delays it.

- Once you've heard your intuition, it doesn't change. In other words, the guidance is the guidance is the guidance is the…, well, you get the message.

Delaying truth always reminds me of a woman in a workshop who bravely and honestly told the group that she knew her marriage was over and was now ready to take action to end it and move on with her life. When I asked her how long she had known this information, she calmly replied, "For thirty years."

It doesn't matter whether you wait thirty years, months, weeks, days, or seconds to act, your life will stay in a perpetual stuck place until you follow the guidance that is right in front of you. This woman had put her life on hold for thirty years. That's a long time to be in limbo.

Her decision to act had a healing effect immediately, and yet all she had done was to own her truth. She left the workshop more energized and much happier and lighter than when the workshop began.

Once you have that intuitive-truth hit, you can't un-know it. You can try to dissociate from it, distract yourself, numb yourself, or get sick, but it doesn't change the guidance. You can burn up a lot of time trying to avoid what you know that you don't want to know, but it still won't change the guidance. You won't be able to move forward until you take that step that is divinely directed for your highest good. Ignoring your truth will make you miserable and leave you on the sidelines of life.

Have you ever noticed that when you ignore guidance, it becomes more obvious, clearer, louder, and more impossible to ignore? Once you secretly know in your heart that you have to break off your engagement, set a boundary, or take a risk, it will press at you until you take action.

As you linger with the information, it takes more and more energy and willpower to turn off your awareness of the flow of information. This is one of the reasons people are so dissociated, not fully present, or get sick. They are ignoring vital information.

You just can't ask for guidance and pretend you didn't get it when you did. Sometimes it takes a lot of spiritual courage to act quickly once you know what you must do, but action at any point in life is better than the continuing stagnation of inaction.

Negotiating your guidance will delay you from a fabulous life.

Ask for a New York sign

Tim had invested a lot of time and money in seminars, books, tapes, and personal coaching to learn to be abundant, but it hadn't worked. During a seminar I *saw* that his physical heart was ill; his energy wasn't behind this path to make money, and he hadn't followed his guidance to move to Hawaii.

This wasn't what Tim wanted to hear. He wasn't about to be deterred from his abundance quest. His wife, however, was listening and at my suggestion prayed for guidance about selling a piece of real estate to raise some cash since their finances were tight. Tim was against the sale; the property was their security blanket for income during lean times.

They were new to the idea of guidance and prayer, so I told Debbie that when she prayed, she should ask for a "New York sign" so there would be no mistaking the fact that she was receiving guidance.

A New York sign is what I call something that stops you in your tracks and forces you to take notice. If you've read my book *Diary of a Medical Intuitive*, you know that I asked for a New York sign at a crucial point in my life, and there was no doubt that I got it. I was literally stopped in my tracks on a narrow path in the Andes.

Debbie asked for a seemingly impossible sign: if her property manager called and quit within two hours of her prayer, she would know it was a sign because she had just spoken to him that morning and he expressed his joy and gratitude for his job. Now this may seem extreme, but remember, her intuition gave her the sign to ask for.

A scant two hours after Debbie prayed for guidance, their property manager called to say he was resigning. Without him, maintaining their investment property would be a huge burden. Within five days, Tim and Debbie were on their way to following their guidance and living their dream.

**A New York sign will stop you in your tracks
so you can move forward.**

Do I need a spirit guide?

Many people don't ask for guidance because they have a concept of God or Higher Power who is big, mysterious, vengeful, and ready to smote them. If that were my belief, I wouldn't ask for help either!

If you are afraid to talk to your Higher Power, one of the most healing things you can do is to explore and rewrite your limiting tribal beliefs about God. This choice will lead to a beneficial and loving communication with the divine realm. (see chapter eight).

When you are afraid of God, or don't feel you are worthy to talk to God, you may find it much easier to ask for help from an intermediary spiritual helper like a guide or an angel who feels less scary to you. However, having a guide is not a requirement for receiving guidance.

Your helpers can come in any shape or size, but will be one that you are innately drawn to because of your experiences and archetypal blueprint. Some folks work with people from the past, others bring in animals, and yet others feel the presence of a loved one who has come to bring them information or comfort.

Remember that the spirit world is not caught up in ego, labels, or appearances. A talking mouse is just as good a companion as an angelic being of light.

If you want a spiritual helper, ask for one to come to you in your dreams or during a meditation, or ask to be sent an angel. It is vitally important that your guide feels loving and safe, has a high vibration, and an open pipeline to the source of unconditional love, forgiveness, and infinite compassion.

Sit quietly and get clear about what you are going to ask your guide to do. Do you really want an answer to your question? Do you really want to feel comfort, reassurance, or strength? Do you really want things to change?

Communicating with your spirit guide is surprisingly easy. There are no special rules. It does not have to be a Sunday, you don't have to be a special person, wear a particular color, or earn the right. You simply call from your heart. Be sincere and you will get a response.

How you receive your help is not important, except that you must request that it come from a high vibration light source. That's why I always address my intentions, prayers, invocations to God, who for me, is unconditional love and the highest vibration of all.

Your guides (and they may change over time), will be known in a way that feels safe for you. While I generally go straight to the top with my requests, I often talk about angels in my teachings because they are a soothing presence for so many people, including myself. I like my guidance to be a comfort, not a hair raising, "who is in my room" experience.

If by chance a guide comes to you who feels uncomfortable, ask for a different form to be shown to you. When a stern, mystical wrinkled Peruvian Indian spirit guide showed up in my room at three in the morning for a chat, I asked him to leave and return in the form of an angel, and at a more decent hour, which he did.

Just as you can ask your guides to show themselves in a form that works for you, you can ask them for exactly what you need, such as guidance or courage, or a parking space on a busy street. Yes, that's right, you can call upon your angels to help you park.

> *Spiritual helpers are up to any request.*
> *Don't get hung up on technicalities;*
> *just ask for help.*

Chapter Three

INTUITIVE DREAMS

Dreaming can be one the most restful ways to receive information; the knowledge will still be succinct and clear. Please don't make the mistake of getting a dream book to understand the symbolism of things like water in your dreams.

Don't get distracted. The same guidance rules apply, whether you get your information from a voice in your head, an inner knowing, a skywriter behind your eyes, or a dream: it's short and sweet and to the point.

Pay attention to what you feel, what you learned, how the story relates to you, and all obvious information. As Bill learned, guidance dreams just don't need a lot of interpretation.

Bill had invested a sum of money and was wondering if he should take out his profits and move on to buy different stocks. The investment had done okay, but not great, and he thought maybe it was time to pull out his money. He thought about the question as he fell asleep, asking that he be shown what to do.

That night he dreamed he was in his garden harvesting some of his vegetables. He noticed that the carrots had been replaced by quarters and bent down to pick them up. At that moment his wife appeared in the garden and admonished him not to disturb the quarters, that if he left them, they would grow larger. As she spoke, the quarters changed to dollar bills.

Bill left his money in the investment which was the smartest thing to do. It did appreciate in value making him more profit, something that wouldn't have happened had he harvested his principle too soon.

Sarah was trying to decide if she should move or stay in her house, but she couldn't come to a decision even after making a long list of the pros and cons. I suggested she tap into her intuition by asking for the information to come in a dream. That night she dreamed she was on an ocean liner that was sinking, and an announcement came over the loudspeaker for everyone to leave the ship and get into a lifeboat immediately.

Do I need to say more?

Life-saving dreams

Help and direction can come in your dreams, and sometimes it just may save a life.

As you know, I was working as an E.R. nurse when I was clearly given guidance to quit my job and use my intuitive gifts full-time. The problem was I didn't want to. For a while, I negotiated with God by keeping my job but doing intuitive readings on the side. I received great satisfaction from my E.R. work, had climbed the ladder of success, and didn't want to jump down from it.

From the outside, it probably looked as if things were going great in my life. But they weren't. Although I loved nursing, I didn't derive life-enhancing energy from my job anymore. There was a nursing shortage at the time, and I went home each night feeling drained from having to make so many difficult life-or-death choices on every shift.

The pivotal event for me was a night shift when a five-year-old with epiglottis in extremis (the airway is blocked due to swelling) was brought in. Literally one minute later, a fifty-five-year-old man with a lethal cardiac arrhythmia arrived. Both conditions are life-threatening, both require immediate one-on-one care, and both patients would die without intervention.

Unfortunately, there was only one E.R. physician and one RN – me. The rest of the staff there that night were unlicensed aides. Life-threatening conditions initially require at least two licensed professionals to stabilize a patient; aides are not qualified to give medications, triage, or perform life-saving interventions other than CPR.

So I did the only thing I could: I told an aide to push the cardiac-arrest alarm in both patients' rooms, knowing that it would awaken all the residents sleeping upstairs. It worked, and both patients pulled through.

What I didn't do was listen to the intuitive message that came that night: *You can't do this job anymore; the situation is untenable and it is draining your vital energy.* Since I ignored my angels, they had to amp up the signal.

After that stressful night, I began to have a recurring dream, which I named the Blood Lake dream. In the dream I was on a bus with many people. Suddenly the bus stopped at a lake and we all got off. There were two paths around the lake. Many people took the path to the right. As I started to follow them, a man with kind eyes pointed to the left and told me to go the other way.

Mesmerized by the aura of love surrounding this man, I turned and went with him toward the left-hand path. Suddenly I heard a moan coming from the right. As a nurse, I felt compelled to find out what was wrong and offer my assistance. When I stepped away from the kind man, he gently took hold of my arm and shook his head, "No." He gestured for me to continue down the left-hand path. I felt torn and then I heard the moan again, much louder this time.

I apologized to the kind man and started walking to the right. The sadness I saw in his eyes was so deep; the memory of it haunts me to this day. As I walked away, I couldn't shake the feeling of his eyes on my back, but I strode determinedly toward the right-hand path around the lake. The moans and wails of suffering became louder and more pitiful. The farther I walked the less color I saw, as everything became a dull gray.

I reached the person who was moaning. He was severely injured and in great pain. His wounds were bleeding profusely and draining into the lake. It was then that I realized the lake was filled with blood. As I tended to the wounded man, I heard more moans and cries for help. The pain and agony of the other injured people echoed across the lake.

Each time I would stop to help someone, another victim would cry out in need. There was no one to help me so I began triaging the best I could, aiding those who seemed most likely to survive and leaving the most desperately wounded to their fate.

The number of victims increased, their pain was extreme, and I knew I could no longer decide to help one and not another. In anguish, I cried out, "I can't play

God!" I couldn't decide who should be helped and who shouldn't, who would have his pain relieved and who wouldn't.

Suddenly I saw an escalator on the path. I jumped on and rode it upward. The higher I went the more color returned to my dream. When I stepped off the escalator I found myself in the middle of Macy's department store, surrounded by colorful and festive Christmas decorations. There were carolers, exquisite gifts, and tinseled trees all around me. It was the biggest Christmas display I had ever seen. In that moment of joy and relief, I awoke from my dream.

I know now that the kind man in my dream was an angel trying to steer me in the direction that was in my highest good. I know this because I recognized the love for me in his eyes and the sadness he felt when I ignored him. The Christmas display inside of Macy's was a metaphor for the peace and joy I would have in my life if I left Blood Lake (the E.R.) and followed my guidance.

At the time, though, this dream both mystified me and shook me to my core. *How could I choose who got help and who didn't without violating my soul?* I prayed to understand the dream's meaning. The message was obvious, of course, but because I didn't want to hear it, I didn't hear it. Instead I distracted myself by analyzing the escalator ride and Christmas at Macy's, looking for symbols.

I continued to ignore the obvious and the dream continued for months and then years. The dream became so frequent and so stressing that one night I prayed to be relieved of it. My prayer was answered, but not quite in the way I had hoped for.

That night I had a dream that left me more traumatized than a car crash. I dreamed I fell one hundred stories down an elevator shaft and died. When I awoke, I was lying on the floor of my room, unable to move or open my eyes. It felt as though every bone in my body was broken. In this "road kill" state I heard a booming voice ordering, "QUIT THE E.R. AND USE YOUR GIFTS FULL-TIME!"

I didn't. The Blood Lake dream returned with a vengeance. The more I tried to negotiate with God so I could stay in the E.R., the more I had the dream. Sometimes I would awake in a cold sweat, feeling completely wrung out from all the triaging I had been forced to do at the lake's edge. Exhausted, I would pray for help. But I always heard the same response. God never wavered. Over and over, the voice said, *Leave your job.* Eventually I listened.

My angels had worked tirelessly to get me to see the light. When I didn't heed their message in my waking life, they came to me in my dreams. Once I finally listened to my guidance and embraced my intuitive gifts full-time, I began walking a path (the left-hand one, no doubt) that has brought me tremendous peace and joy. My life still has occasional bumps in the road, but mostly, every day feels like Christmas.

Dreams of warning

Our dreams, while not always pleasant, should not be under valued. They can be a warning of imminent danger, a portent of what is to come, an answer to a prayer, or simply another way of sending us guidance. Fortunately, I am not always that obtuse about the messages from my angels that arrive in dreams – even if the dreams are someone else's.

On my last day of vacation in the Bahamas, I decided to go parasailing. For some reason, I called home to check in. I found my mom rather distracted, only half listening to my adventures.

"What's wrong?" I asked. She took a deep breath and began, "I had a strange dream and I don't understand it. There was a multicolored…I don't know…it looked like a parachute floating in the air. Then I saw a rope dangling."

The hair on my arms stood up as she spoke.

"It really shook me up," she said. "Please don't go near anything like that, okay?"

I hung up. A chill climbed up my spine. It sounded like she'd seen the bright colors of a parasail that had lost its rider. Then my skeptical, rational mind kicked in, and I went to the beach anyway. I watched a man who was strapped into the harness of a parasail rise effortlessly into the sky, and I reveled at the thought of flying like that. I wanted to know what it felt like.

But something inside held me back; my mother's dream had gotten to me. In the next instant, I saw that the wind had kicked up, and the men driving the parasail towboat were trying to pull their rider quickly back to shore. Suddenly the guide rope broke, and the man in the harness dangled like a rag doll in the hand of a running child.

I watched in horror as the wind swept him into the side wall of the hotel. His chute crumpled and he fell several hundred feet to his death. It was a devastating moment that taught me to be respectful of all intuitive information that comes to me.

My mother had already learned this lesson, so when I had a prophetic dream warning of danger to her, she didn't hesitate to listen. I awoke one day in a cold sweat from the second most vivid dream in my life: I watched in horror as my mom crossed a street and was hit by a white car.

I saw her fly across the hood and smash into the ground. I heard the roar of the speeding car and the terrible sound of her bones breaking. I felt like I was inside her as her blood seeped onto the pavement. I felt pain, then no pain. She was dead.

I grabbed the phone and called her at the condo where my parents were vacationing in Hawaii, even though it was only 5:00 a.m. there.

"Well, hi," she said brightly. "You just caught me. I was on my way out the door."

"Don't go outside," I screamed. Words tumbled breathlessly from my mouth. I described the street I had seen in my dream, the surrounding buildings, and the sidewalk. Even though I had never been to Hawaii and knew nothing about the condo my parents had rented, my description was completely accurate.

"But why don't you want me to go outside?" my mother asked.

"Because I saw you crossing that street and being hit by a car."

Silence filled the line. Finally my mother said in a small voice, "Every morning I go across the street to buy the morning paper. I was just opening the door to go when you called."

Chapter Four

YOU CAN'T RUN OUT OF MIRACLES

Some people believe that guides have much more important things to do than help humans find parking spaces. That's like believing that a St. Bernard should only rescue good or worthy people. A St. Bernard doesn't care and doesn't judge whether you are a hapless soul, a fool, a daredevil, or had an unfortunate accident before coming to your rescue. They just come. Every call for help matters to them. Even yours.

The idea that an angel would judge you or your request for help is absurd. Your request is not forwarded to the Angel Committee and a vote taken on its worthiness. Their function is simply to help you. No job is too big or too small.

I was late for a book signing in upstate New York and came flying through the lobby when I noticed a group of women waiting for a taxi. They had been waiting over half an hour and they too were late for my book signing. I turned around and loaded them into my car saying, "don't worry about being late. They can't start without me."

When we arrived at the overflowing parking lot, the back seat said in unison, "Let's call the parking angel." It was music to my ears as we easily parked.

If you think that your spiritual helpers should intervene only when it's really important, or that you can only ask for help twice per week, you are running a real risk of living in spiritual scarcity.

Your thoughts and attitude play a large role in your spiritual life. You can create an abundance of miracles in your life by asking for help whenever you need it, and accepting it when it comes.

Listen and watch carefully for all the amazing doors put in front of you and all the wonderful possibilities that come your way, including an abundance of people in your life who don't make fun of your beliefs and who support your spiritual openness.

Your intuition is available all the time, your spirit guides are always ready to help you, and you can put yourself in the flow at any time. Make a request, keep an open heart, and say thank you, even to the parking angels who keep you from being late.

Spiritual scarcity limits the miracles in your life.
Help will come as many times as you need,
even for the same problem.

The Italian Angel

Once you have asked for help, then what? I said earlier that hearing your intuition requires you to be open to help and sincere in your request. That's true. But when the help arrives, you also have to open your eyes and your mind or you'll miss it. You can become so focused on your own agenda that you miss the help when it comes. Now you are out of the flow.

I confess to having done this during a spiritual pilgrimage to Italy. At the Rome train station, Rebecca and I bought tickets to Assisi, home of St. Francis. Railway departures are famously precise in Italy. Trains wait for no one, not even women on a spiritual journey.

After checking the track number and time of departure, we waited on Platform 18 for the train. I triple-checked the departures board for the train schedule and the assigned platform as the train pulled in. Everything was in order. But no sooner had we turned to board the train than hundreds of people, seemingly from nowhere filled the platform. We couldn't reach the door of the car, though it was scarcely twenty feet ahead of us. The harder we tried, the more people filled our path. We were trapped.

I knew the train would not wait for us, yet getting to that door felt like a Herculean task. It was more than I could do. I prayed for God to help us board the train on time as I struggled with my rolling suitcase and blustered my way through the crowds until I found another place to climb on board.

Those were the roughest steps I have ever taken. People banged into me, pushed me, and shoved me. Somewhere deep in my brain, this registered as strange. The Italian people are usually so friendly, so polite, yet for all the consideration they were giving us, we could have been invisible.

Finally, we climbed the four steps into the car, sweating but exhilarated to have triumphed in our struggle. Wrong. The aisle ahead was bursting with people moving toward us. Again, something felt wrong. We had boarded through the door at the very head of the train. People should have been moving with us, toward the rear, not against us. Our assigned seats were back in the third car.

Determined I was, so I gathered my strength and courage and forged ahead, hollering to Rebecca, "Follow me!" We didn't get very far. My suitcase caught on everything and everyone. I said, "Excuse me, scusi, HELLOOO," but no one moved, and I could not make my way down the aisle.

Rebecca called out, "Let's get off and try another car." We managed to climb off the train with absolutely no interference, but the platform was as crowded as it had been before. Checking the clock, I saw we had exactly four minutes before the train left.

"Get back on," I shouted, "We'll find the right car after the train settles down."

Up those treacherous stairs we went, struggling with small suitcases that had suddenly become much heavier, bigger, and cumbersome. This would have been a great time to pay attention to what was happening, but I was focused on my goal: boarding the darn train.

Again the aisle was packed – where had all these people come from, and why weren't they in their seats? The train was leaving in two minutes. I took a breath and reminded myself that we had reserved seats and would eventually get to sit down somewhere. I again asked God for help to board the train.

Eventually I let go of any attachment to the outcome of our trip. "It's in your hands," I whispered. Rebecca spotted an opening in the sea of people and went for it. I followed her.

We pushed our way six feet down the aisle when suddenly a large woman in the biggest fur coat I have ever seen came toward us with a look of Viking determination. I don't know what linebackers feel like the first time they are blocked, but that day I had a good idea. This woman meant business.

She and her big fur coat bore down on us and literally pushed us backward toward the door through which we'd entered. All our "scusi's" fell on deaf ears. She pushed us further and further until we were at the steps again. She didn't stop there. Her suitcase rolled over Rebecca's foot and jammed into my side. Her look said, "I'm not finished!"

"That's it," I hollered, "We're out of here. St. Francis is just going to have to wait. Get off the train before it starts moving." We hurried down the steps just as the train began to pull out of the station.

The platform was completely and utterly silent. The crowd had evaporated. On the train itself, no one was standing in the aisles of the car we just left. I got that weird shivery feeling and looked up to see the Viking woman in the fur coat smiling down at me as the train pulled out of the station.

She didn't look so scary; in fact she was somehow comforting. I knew something important had happened, but I was so focused on my agenda of getting to Assisi that, as C.S. Lewis once observed, we are often unaware of the profundity of the moment. Sorely disappointed, we went to the ticket booth for a refund.

"But you will miss the train!" exclaimed the ticket clerk. "Do you not want to go to Assisi?"

"Of course we do. But…" I answered. "Hurry to track eleven," he interrupted. "You have less than three minutes."

As it turned out, the railway authorities had switched the track for the Assisi train and had neglected to update the departures board. The train we had been trying so hard to take was a non-stop express to Milan. Had we succeeded, we would have been trapped on a six-hour 300-mile train journey, stuck in Milan overnight, and missed our connections from Rome the next morning.

I thought of all our struggling and realized that had we gone with the flow – literally – we would never even have gotten aboard that train. I realized that angels had crowded that platform to prevent us from boarding, but because of our determination (or should I say stubbornness), we persisted. I even prayed for help!

My help had arrived in a big fur coat and she could have prevented the entire offensive line of the Dallas Cowboys from taking seats on that train. She had gotten us off the Milan express just in time. I had to laugh. How much more obvious could my guidance have been?

You can become so determined to achieve your goal that you neglect to see all the signs and help that surround you. Your focus becomes so narrow that you can lose sight of the big picture.

The next time you are doing something – preparing a meal, boarding a train, buying a lawn mower, or driving a car, and something feels like it's not working, seems too difficult or is a struggle, look up from your task and ask if you are still on the right track. Your guidance may be trying to tell you to slow down, change direction, stop, or get off.

I had prayed for help to board the train on time and stuck to that prayer like glue. I stuck to this prayer despite clear signs that boarding the train was going to be difficult, and it caused me to fall out of the flow.

Had I let go of my agenda the moment I felt a problem on that train, I would have updated my prayer and asked for guidance on what to do in that moment. I now know that I would have heard, "get off."

Once off the train, I could have asked, "now what," being open to guidance that said, don't go to see St. Francis today, or go somewhere else in Italy today, or go home and rest today, or board a different train.

Because I was so focused on my program, I left little room for divine direction. You need to let go of your program, even if you excitedly planned it all out the night before, and open up to the flow of the moment.

Guidance, like Microsoft updates, comes frequently. Check in more often when what you are doing becomes difficult, or your actions seem continually thwarted.

Synchronicity and the haunted house

Following your intuition can result in unimagined and wonderfully synchronistic events. This was the case one day when I received an interesting call from a realtor who knew about my work in clearing energy from houses. She had a beautiful home listed that though under priced, was simply not selling even though it was gorgeous and in a great location. Her intuition told her to call me.

I knew there was trouble when I touched the handle on the front door. I was frozen in place, flooded with foreboding and dread. The hair on the back of my neck was making that prickly cold feeling and I didn't want to go inside. I asked for guidance and was told to go in.

A friend who describes herself as the "Ray Charles of the energy world" was with me and even she was clearly terrified. Walking into the house felt like walking into a crypt, only the occupants weren't resting in peace. They were malignant and quite angry at my intrusion.

Although we turned on all the lights, the rooms remained dark and cold. I felt eyes upon me and knew the house was haunted. As I moved through the large house, I was acutely aware that malevolent energies had infested every room except the den.

Over the next two days, I did a clearing ceremony, which, while simple in form, should only be undertaken with the greatest of care. The ritual for such a ceremony is quite uncomplicated, and anyone who tells you otherwise either doesn't know what they are talking about or uses the complication to create an aura of expertise or mystery so they feel more powerful.

I first prayed for God's protection and then burned sweet grass and invited all the occupants of the house to a meeting. I needed to know why they were there.

I listened to their complaints, resentments, fears, and their pain. Many of them were stuck in a low vibration because of their need for vengeance, a "poor me" victim attitude, and an unwillingness to forgive themselves or others. Know that the energies that you live by in this life, will also contaminate you in the afterlife if you don't heal them on either plane.

The bulk of my time was spent healing the houseguests. Those who healed went willingly into the light; those who refused to raise their vibration were commanded in the name of God, for them and all their negativity to leave the home and to return to the light.

I feel it is important to command such energies back to the light, because I don't want them roaming around the universe, ready to resonate and join with any negativity in this realm. It's always their choice and even though they don't always take it, I like to give them another chance to align with the light.

When you command a low vibration spirit, energy, or entity to leave you or a physical location, you must mean it with all your heart. There cannot be a part of you that is fascinated with seeing what that darkness is really like or a part that is fearful of being contaminated.

As the vibration of the home raised, I became aware of other powerful and benevolent energies in the den, there to protect, soften, and balance the land. I then filled the home with God's light, love, and protection.

You will experience, as I did in that house, a lifting of the heaviness, a feeling of movement, and a sense of warmth. You will feel happy, light, and at ease, and the house will feel different and indeed, it will be different. Oh yes, and your friend's hair will stop protruding at right angles to her head!

Thinking that my work was done, I walked through the magnificent home to feel the changes and experience the results of God's grace in that dwelling. But as I entered the living room, I heard such a distinct cry for help that I instinctively turned toward it before I realized it had been spoken on the etheric plane, not the physical realm.

I turned my attention to the voice and received a clear message that there was a woman connected with the house between thirty-five and forty who was in urgent need of medical help. I knew it was not the owner, but there was a connection with the house that was strong and persistent. Again, I was told the need was urgent, that this woman needed an appointment with her gynecologist and had to have a pap smear immediately.

As I recounted this information to the realtor, she mentioned the caretaker of the house. She made a call and handed me the phone. I knew after two words that this was not the woman I was looking for, but when I spoke with her thirty-eight-year-old daughter I knew she was the one.

I explained the urgency of the message given to me and said she needed to see her doctor right away, and if her test came back okay, to have it repeated. The daughter was puzzled since she had had a clean pap smear six weeks earlier and wasn't due for another one for at least a year. Furthermore, she felt fine, had no symptoms, and would normally not have returned to her doctor since there was nothing wrong.

Nonetheless, she listened to me, and insisted that her puzzled physician do another pap smear. The results showed a frightening and aggressive cancer for which she had immediate and life saving surgery.

As for the house, the owner decided to keep it in the family and took it off the market. I think they just liked the way it felt without all the extra energies floating around.

You might not always be told why you are guided to do something, but do it anyway.

Chapter Five

GUIDANCE AND GRACE

Simply put, grace is help from God that we receive just because we asked for it.

It's important for you to know that none of the things I am telling you comes from the tenets of any particular religion. What I know about God and how God's love works is based on my actual experience. Because I have traveled to the other side and seen spiritual beings of light, I know they exist. I know they will come whenever you ask for help and are with you when you die. This is fact, whether you choose to believe it or not.

If you need to argue or debate the truth of these statements, I would ask, "Why do you want to work so hard to disprove something so good?" You have a choice where you invest your energy. Doesn't it make more sense to try out the truth of what I'm saying than to waste your energy on debate or excuses?

I did a reading for Ken, a fifty-seven-year-old man with lung cancer. On the deepest level, he knew he was dying, but consciously he chose to ignore this and was working full-time. Ken's vibration was low, not only from the illness, but because he was disconnected from God and spiritually adrift.

Ken had been angry with God when he was diagnosed with cancer, but now he just felt resigned to his fate. He had no connection with God, and I was saddened by the emptiness I saw inside him. Ken did not have that much time left here on earth, and I knew that his transition would be gentler and easier if he could reconnect with God before he went. It was time for some spiritual guidance.

Ken and I prayed together and in my mind's eye, I saw a picture of him with a big grin on his face driving to various truck stops and ordering all kinds of pie. I didn't understand the guidance, but I told Ken what I saw.

His eyes filled with tears as a broad smile spread across his face. "How could you know," he began, "that my dream is to eat at truck stops around the country and find the best pie?"

His family and friends knew Ken as a connoisseur of pie, and he loved to share the great pie destinations he discovered. In fact, he had often thought of writing the ultimate pie book.

It was clear that Ken's guidance was to allow himself some joy. This may seem like a simple task, but for some people it's not. When you get this kind of guidance, it's

God's way of saying, "You are loved, you are important, you deserve joy and happiness."

That afternoon Ken opened himself to God and wept. He understood now that he was loved and would not die alone He could fulfill his dream of going on the great American pie hunt.

Most people don't understand that being happy is a way of being of service to others. Ken's situation reminded me of Johnny Appleseed. Whereas Johnny spread apple trees throughout the world, Ken would spread his high vibration, his joy, his contagious laughter and happiness, and the knowledge that having a difficult illness does not mean you have to stop living. Ken would also spread the message that being of service can be fun – it can even involve eating apple pie.

When I pray with people, what I hear is their priority task – the single most important thing they can do right now to heal, and something that, when accomplished, will untangle a myriad of other problems.

Who would have thought someone's priority task could be so much fun? But the truth is I've listened to some great guidance while praying with others over the years. It included, "Learn to cook, go shopping, quit your job, leave your relationship, move to Hawaii," and, of course, "Eat pie!"

Celebrate your healing

While your guidance can come in many different ways, it always leaves you feeling better than before it came. This was especially true for me one June day in New York.

One morning shortly after I'd finished college, I awoke to find the novel I had spent three years writing wiped clean from my computer. Even my backup disk was blank.

I prayed to recover my precious book from whatever limbo it had gone into, but nothing happened. It had vanished without logical explanation.

I lay on the couch in my basement apartment in black despair, thinking about all the hard work that had been wasted. A part of my soul had gone into that book, and losing it felt like a traumatic amputation. I wondered if I would ever write again. In my despair, all I could pray was "help."

Suddenly, a stranger in a blue and white striped shirt appeared at my screen door. I didn't know him, but he seemed so familiar I never thought to be afraid. His kind eyes drew me in, and I suddenly felt bathed in a pool of comfort. His smile was so warm and infectious, I found myself smiling back at him as I sat up.

It still had not struck me that a strange man was standing there, but I was aware of how different I felt – how wondrously hopeful. I floated in the comfort he brought as he spoke just a few words.

"It will be okay, you will write again."

I stared at him, not certain if he had actually spoken or if I had heard the words in my mind. When he turned to leave, I felt like all hope and love were being wrenched away. I jumped up from the couch and ran to the door. He was climbing the stairs to the driveway.

"Wait! What's your name?"

He turned and smiled. "Tom," he replied softly, and then continued on his way.

Hearing his name stopped me in my tracks momentarily as confusion, *who was this guy at my door and how did he know about my writing?* and comfort because he felt familiar, and excitement because deep inside I realized that something profound was occurring.

I threw open the door and raced up the short flight of steps…only to find him completely gone. Behind him, though, Tom had left a definite imprint on me – one of joy, hope, and strength.

I puzzled over this man. Who was he? How did he know I was sad? Why was he so darn familiar? It felt like I had received a gift, and I savored it even though I could make little sense of the encounter.

Shortly thereafter, I began to write again but in a very different way. My writing came more from my gut and my heart rather than my intellect. Expressing myself this way felt right and comfortable and true, and it still does to this day.

I have since learned that because of my electromagnetic energy, I tend to wreak havoc on computers; they frequently crash without warning, lose data inexplicably, or I cause very strange happenings within them that baffle the computer experts. I also learned that I tend to cause major malfunctions in most things of an electronic nature, and therefore limit my exposure to them, for their protection, not mine!

Years later, I mentioned my experience to one of my aunts. We were talking about God, and I said I was sure an angel had been sent to intervene in my life just when I needed one. When I described my apartment and my visit from "Tom the angel," as I always thought of him, my aunt became very quiet. Then she began to weep.

"What's wrong?" I ventured. "This was a great experience – it changed my life. Why are you crying?"

"I miss my father," she said quietly.

Then she took a deep breath and told me a story. It turned out that my aunt had lived in the same exact apartment at the same exact age I had. During this time she was in a period of deep sadness from missing her father, my grandfather, who had died. She felt so alone and without direction in life.

One night, while lying awake in bed crying and staring at the ceiling, she prayed for help. She felt a soothing presence on her shoulders, and was instantly comforted and filled with hope. She dried her tears and fell into a peaceful slumber.

I thought it was an interesting story. We had both lived in the same place at the same age. We had both asked for help and were brought great comfort at a time of great need. And we had both had such a profound feeling of peace, strength, and hope that we knew something miraculous had occurred.

But that wasn't the end of the story.

"Christel, you were very young when your grandfather died," my aunt said, taking my hand, "so you might not remember this, but his name was Tom – and he loved his blue and white striped shirts."

"Tom" taught me that we can heal our hearts fast by opening to the divine. I have no doubt he was sent to me to bring me comfort and hope during a time of temptation to feel hopeless. Angels or spiritual guides rescue us from our humanness, and prevent us from parking in a low vibration attitude or mood.

You do need rescuing when you languish in feeling unworthy, undeserving, or beaten down. These moments create an illusion that you are separate from God.

Angels demolish that illusion. When your own erroneous beliefs or pride start to isolate you from love, they fan the spark of light in your soul until it becomes a blazing fire, and you can't help but be reminded of the divine.

You are blessed to have spiritual helpers who are not concerned with the needs of your ego, your wealth, IQ, or need for power, only your highest good. Without them, you would get lost in the illusion of separation and drift easily because of all the distractions that catch your eye.

Spiritual helpers are a gift of grace. They understand your spirit because it is an extension of the brilliant light that connects all of us to the divine. They help you to remember who you really are.

If you allow it, your spirit can bring balance to your world when you need it most. There is a flame of inspiration that burns deeply and steadfastly within you; it is the hallmark of your spirit and always there, and will leave you feeling joyous, content, creative, or with a sense of peace deep within.

Such moments of grace come as unexpected and delightful surprises, but some manifest because you have reached out and asked for them. This was the case with a woman who was hurting because her ex-husband was spreading malicious lies about her several years after their divorce.

She prayed for guidance and asked, "What should I do about him?" The answer she got was, "Stay focused on God." This seemed like a strange answer to her because it didn't seem to address the problem.

But her guidance was right on. The woman's real problem was not her ex-husband's lies. It was her attachment to her reputation. His lies were distressing her because she was concerned that other people would believe them. She thought that her worth depended on her reputation, and his lies would diminish her in the eyes of others.

This was exactly the problem the angels addressed when they replied, "Stay focused on God." When the woman focused on God, she felt God's love for her and knew her real worth. She was able to reconnect with her spirit and embrace her true nature. This has allowed her to be of service to others and have an extremely positive ripple effect on those around her.

She was able to spread love rather than resentment. Had she focused on anything but God when she felt damaged by her ex-husband's lies, her sense of low self-worth would not have been addressed and her ripple effect on others would have been one of shame, worry, and anger.

The guidance you receive may come at a much higher vibration than your request, so it may be hard to recognize, understand, or accept at first.

Trust your spiritual experiences

Synchronistic healing moments can either help you align with your true passionate nature, or make you nervous because they happen so effortlessly and in quick succession. To alleviate your worry, it helps to remember a few things about the world of intuition and guidance:

- It is always available to you, no matter what you have said or done in the past.

- Synchronistic events, (you might call them coincidences) occur all the time, whether you believe in them or not.

- When you are in the flow, things do happen quickly and effortlessly. Try to receive them graciously.

- Your sixth sense is much smarter than you are.

- Intuition doesn't always seem to make sense, but it can always be trusted.

When your intuition demands big changes in your life, it's almost impossible not to think of the people who will be affected by your choices. A good example is when you receive the intuition to leave a relationship. Your thoughts go to your partner, the hurt, and the upheaval, delaying your decision, and slowing down your guidance.

But how do you know if leaving your partner isn't the best thing for them? You don't always see the bigger picture, but your intuition is based on a spiritual perspective, much wider than your human view.

The view from your car when a driver cuts you off, might leave you with anger or driving righteousness, eager to let him know what a lousy driver he is. The incident becomes focused on you and your judgment of the situation.

A spiritual perspective keeps in mind that the man might be rushing to his wife's side in the hospital; that he cut you off because he was distracted by his fear and grief over her condition.

I'm not telling you to be spiritually groovy and to always make excuses for people's bad behavior. Let's face it, sometimes people are just jerks, and there is no hospitalized spouse involved. You can still ask for help in remaining calm, preserving your high vibration, moving forward without losing your power, and holding on to your precious psychic energy. It's okay to get mad, but don't park there.

When you have a more intimate relationship with something outside of *your* physical world, you will learn that:

- Spiritual helpers are messengers from God bringing hope and reminding you of your true spiritual nature.

- Your intuition will change you for the better and give you much to be grateful for.

- Guidance can bring daily miracles into your life.

- Listening to your spirit will transform you into a better person, and guide you away from your ego, so you can heal your pride and old wounds.

- You are never alone.

Intuition, your pipeline to the spiritual world, will protect, guide, warn, teach, comfort, and give you the courage and inspiration to be a better person.

Ask for help in making a decision, guidance on what to do next, comfort from your despair, or whatever else you need help with. Sometimes your request will be specific, such as "Should I take this job?"

Other times you may simply feel stuck or lost, and need to reclaim a dose of positivity, but don't know how to phrase your need.

Using the *Christel Cards: Prayers to Raise Your Vibration* is a great way to get started. The prayers are specially written to create movement in your life toward a higher purpose. You can use them to confirm your inner knowing and help you stay focused on your intentions. One of the prayers is called *Unstuck*:

Fill me with determination, lift me from discouragement, and set me on course toward an answer that works. Inspire me with ideas and possibilities, and focus my thoughts on hope and solutions. Amen.

Your highest good doesn't mean something bad for someone else.

Angels in the E.R.

Have you ever run into someone who said exactly the thing you needed to hear? Sometimes it's an angel bringing comfort to your heart. Angels don't always take human form, but when they do, the scenario is always the same: the person who prayed sees, talks with, or is helped by someone who suddenly "disappears" and can't be found again. Physical descriptions of these angels are vague, but the wonderful feelings associated with their arrival are powerful and imprint us for life.

Seeing an angel is something you will never forget. Just conjuring the image of the Italian Angel in the fur coat leaves me breathless with laughter, and is a reminder not to focus so much on my agenda, but allow myself to be guided. Picturing Tom the angel always reminds me of the infinite love and comfort available to me during those nasty bumps in the road of life.

Angels are seen in other ways too. If you've ever had a near death experience, it's likely you've seen at least one angel. When I cross over with people, the space is so crowded with angels that their light is at once brilliant and almost blinding.

Having an angel whisper in your ear can be just as comforting. That happened one snowy night in January. I was driving a friend home when we hit a patch of black ice and I lost control of the car.

"Help us! Protect us! Keep us safe!" I prayed. I spun the wheel in the proper direction to stop our skid, but it didn't work. We fishtailed back and forth across the busy two lane highway. I should have been scared as we slid toward the tangle of cars directly in our path, but suddenly, I had an unusual feeling like a breath of cold air upon my neck that made me shiver. Then I heard a voice in my head say, "It will be okay."

In my mind's eye, I saw in slow motion the five car accident in front of me that was about to happen. Even though I was powerless to change anything, I did not panic. I knew before the first car crashed that we would not be injured. In fact, I knew we would not be one of the five vehicles in the accident even though there were cars skidding on ice all around us.

Somehow, my Honda was protected and cradled as we passed straight through the chaos of cars slamming into each other and spinning out of control across both lanes of traffic. White-knuckled and wheezing, my friend turned to stare back at the devastation on the road behind us.

The next day she asked me, "Why didn't you panic when it looked like we were going to crash? Was it because of your E.R. training?"

"No," I replied. "It was because my intuition told me not to worry because we'd make it through safely." To me it was so natural to hear an angel's voice in my head that I didn't stop to consider the impact of my explanation on my friend. She later acknowledged she had thought I was really weird at the time, but she did want to know more about angels.

Angels are vibrant, humorous, and powerful, and know where they are needed. I cannot count the number of times I saw angels visiting the people I nursed during my sixteen years as an E.R. and trauma nurse in New York. The more open you are to receiving their help, the easier it is to be aware of them.

Children often have an easier time seeing angels because they haven't been taught to ignore or fear them. Children accept angels and spiritual guides as a natural part of life. As indeed they are.

Even if you don't actually see an angel, there will be physical cues, like a slight shiver, or a voice inside of your head. You can recognize an angel at work when you find yourself doing something kind or saying something wise that seems a bit out of character, and you wonder, "Where did that come from?"

Having an angel with you doesn't mean you'll escape accidents, injury, or death. But you will have a sense of calm, peace, and ease no matter how a situation plays out. You will face your challenges without being alone. And not being alone during a trial can make all the difference. This was profoundly evident the night baby Joseph was brought into my emergency room.

While working in the E.R., we often saw terrible tragedies – the deaths of children and parents, loss of limbs, gunshot and knife wounds, and the pain and suffering of those afflicted with illness.

One evening in the E.R. was particularly difficult. Four-month-old baby Joseph was brought in without breath or heartbeat. I knew he would not survive and would be met on the other side by a slew of angels, so instead of praying for him, I prayed for an angel for his mother.

She was in shock and could barely stand as the huge stretcher carrying her tiny, utterly still baby was rolled into the E.R. The E.R. staff dropped everything and prepared for baby Joseph.

Nurses and doctors lined every inch of the stretcher, from top to bottom. Their anxious faces intensified as the hospital operator announced a Pediatric Code Blue over the P.A. system.

Prayers were silently whispered, oaths were sworn, and each of us sucked in air and held it when we saw the infant. Babies are supposed to be pink and cute, but baby Joseph was blue and bloated.

With two huge fingers, a doctor was pressing on the baby's chest, squeezing the heart between sternum and backbone. A tube thinner than a straw was inserted into his little mouth and down his trachea to bring oxygen to his breathless lungs, but it was all to no avail.

I took the dreaded walk to find his mother. She wasn't hard to spot among the twenty to thirty people in the waiting room. Her gaze was glued to me, anxious for my eyes to meet hers. Those last few steps across the room to her side were the worst. I wanted to take her to the privacy of the Quiet Room and talk to her there, preserving the dignity of her grief, but it was not to be.

At first baby Joseph's mother thought I was being nice and just giving her a break from the crowd in the waiting room. But I knew that when she went into that room, she would lose her son, and soon she knew it too. She hesitated in the doorway, pierced my soul with her eyes, and would go no further.

In giving her the bad news about her baby, I was supposed to follow a script and start by gently inferring that the boy's situation was grave, even though in reality there was no hope for him. I was supposed to break the news slowly, but I knew I was evading the truth, and my eyes betrayed me.

"Tell me," she whispered. "Tell me the truth."

I silently shook my head no, and she collapsed into my arms. Wrenching sobs tore through her body, as the doctor spotted us. He motioned for me to take the woman into the Quiet Room, but I raised my eyebrows, indicating defeat. Then the woman lifted her head from my shoulder.

Mascara had run down both cheeks and she looked utterly helpless. I wrapped my arm protectively around her shoulders and squeezed as the doctor began his rehearsed lines.

He told her that baby Joseph's heart still wouldn't beat on its own, and explained how the brain begins to die when deprived of oxygen for longer than four minutes. Then he claimed he didn't know what the outcome would be.

The woman took a deep breath and asked if her son was dying. The doctor gave a pat reply about doing everything he could.

"I want to hold his hand," she said. "I don't want him to die alone."

I nodded my head and the doctor shot me a warning look. He advised her against it and started to leave. When I opened my mouth to protest, he silenced me with a glare.

I left the woman weeping into her hands and returned to the Code Room. No progress had been made as CPR continued on baby Joseph; that little heart just refused to beat. I moved close to the doctor and told him in a low voice that the mother had the right to be with her baby. He looked at me with disbelieving eyes and asked if I could really subject her to this sight.

I looked at the blue and bloated form on the stretcher but all I saw was a dying child who needed his mother.

I returned to baby Joseph's mother. I knew she was determined to see her child, and I felt she had the right to be with him.

I prayed for an angel to be with her, to comfort her and bring her strength. I knew that baby Joseph would be met in the afterlife; in fact, angels already surrounded him. It was her I was worried about.

I brought the woman to her baby's side. I explained the tubes and the procedures that were going on. She sat quietly holding his tiny hand, oblivious to the crowd of doctors and nurses and aides, the blood on the sheets, and those two huge fingers pushing on that tiny chest. She looked to the doctor, asking silently if there was any hope.

He shrugged his shoulders and gave the scripted reply, "We're doing everything we can."

At that instant I felt a surge in the air and something changed – baby Joseph's mother shifted from shock and despair to an almost ethereal calm. She looked as though she were listening to someone whispering in her ear. I found out later that she had prayed for an angel at the very same moment I had.

She had been painfully torn between wanting us to continue life-saving measures and telling us to stop the CPR. She knew deep down there was no hope, but she couldn't bear to be the one who ended her child's life. So she had asked for an angel to help her be strong and take loving care of her baby.

Suddenly the room took on a shimmer of energy that signaled an answer to her prayer. She glanced at the doctor as if she were seeing him for the first time. Her face changed, and I could see strength in her that had not been there before. She said she didn't want her baby to suffer anymore, and asked the doctor to stop CPR.

Several faces expressed shock, but she didn't see them. She never took her eyes from baby Joseph. The doctor tried to convince her to rethink her decision, but she only shook her head and said she couldn't allow any more suffering.

The room seemed to divide in that instant between those who agreed with her and those who felt she was giving up too soon – this was a baby boy, after all, not a ninety-nine-year-old man.

Everyone looked to the doctor to see what he would do, when suddenly the mother reached out and gently took the big hand doing CPR into her own, and said, "Please, no more."

Time slowed as her words lingered. No one moved or spoke. Even if there had been a gun at each of our heads, none of us would have restarted the CPR.

I watched baby Joseph's spirit rise from his body in glorious freedom. For an instant he hovered in that room and then was gone. Oddly, it was almost beautiful.

"It was the angel," she told me later, "that steadied my hand to stop CPR. I didn't think I had the strength to do it and suddenly I saw myself doing it."

No one spoke but I noticed a few raised eyebrows. The disbelievers had shown themselves. I asked everyone to leave the room before I bathed baby Joseph.

For more than an hour his mother rocked him on her breast, quietly whispering sweet nothings. It was an angel that brought her peace with her decision, and an angel that gave her hope that she would make it through this terrible ordeal.

Sometimes terrible and stressful things happen in our lives or to those you love, but you never have to feel alone or abandoned and can always ask for comfort, strength, or peace to ease your grief.

Chapter Six

STAY TRUE TO WHAT YOU KNOW

I know that some people believe there are important angels and lesser angels, but my experiences say otherwise. When you die, beings of light or angels comfort you and escort you to "the room" where you are enveloped in light and suffused with joy. When I travel with the dying and stand at the threshold to this room, I can see that light inside and every angel is the same.

No one angel is brighter, bigger, or more powerful than another is. There is no receiving line or pecking order of angels. The light beckons the dying to enter, add their light to the celestial community, and immerse themselves in God's love.

Having seen that there are no greater or lesser angels, when I pray for help I don't measure the size of the job and request an accordingly sized angel. I ask for help and receive it. If you get lost in trying to understand an angelic hierarchy, getting help will become a complicated process for you, delaying any intervention. Just ask.

While angels do not have assigned jobs, our interactions with them feel different because our needs are different, and our needs do have a hierarchy. For example, when you are granted a small blessing, like finding a parking space in a crowded town, or being helped to arrive at an important interview on time, it's like listening to a wave lapping against the shore of a secluded lake. The experience leaves you feeling happy and grateful.

On the other hand, when an angel comforts you and lifts your despair, or replaces your sadness with joy, it's like being scrubbed clean and polished after being covered in mud. You feel like you are glistening with glory.

When you hear, feel, or see an angel, your spirit rejoices. Seeing an angel imprints you for life. It is an experience you will never forget, the memory of which will always bring you comfort, tears, laughter, or some other strong emotional response.

Being visited by an angel or spirit guide goes deeper than anything else we have experienced in the context of our humanness. We are encountering the spirit of unconditional love and the energy of true forgiveness.

But please resist the urge to downplay the angel who parks your car because I have news for you. The angel that magnificently transports someone to the afterlife this evening was parking somebody's car this morning.

You may find that believing in spirit helpers or living your life based on your beliefs gets you "kicked out" of your numerous tribes - your family, teachers, and religious institutions. But angels will still take care of you.

Angels love you unconditionally even when others do not. In fact, angels love you even when you are not sure you love yourself. I learned this valuable lesson one evening in July many years ago.

While slowly coming into acceptance of my intuitive gifts, I struggled with my relationship with the Catholic Church, in which I had been raised. According to the church, seeing the future or having gifts such as clairvoyantly seeing where illness is in the body, reading someone's energy field or aura, and viewing a running "video" of their past is an abomination.

Activities like these are considered profoundly evil. I knew that accepting the truth of my gifts and deciding to use them, even for good, would make me an outcast in my church. When we break the rules of our tribe and decide to leave it, we are never given a cake brightly inscribed with "Congratulations on leaving the tribe!" Rather, it's a time of rejection – or worse.

In a moment of indecision, I went to speak to a priest about my dilemma: was I evil or was I blessed? Our conversation was quite brief. When I began to outline my problem, he quickly stood and raised his arm, index finger pointing at me as though warding off evil. "Get out!" he roared. "You are demon spawn. Never return to the church."

These are intense words to hear when you have just turned twenty-one, but they did not devastate me (though needless to say, I did not step one foot in a Catholic church for a long, long time). I know my angels stood with me that day, hands upon my shoulders, protecting me from the full brunt of the priest's betrayal.

The pain of that rejection could have devastated me, creating doubts and fears, and causing me to abandon my gifts. It did not. My angelic helpers made it clear that my intuition was a gift from God, and therefore it couldn't be evil. They made it clear that I was loved regardless of what this man said and regardless of how the tribe reacted to my God-given gift. I became grateful instead of fearful, and my wound began to heal quickly.

Eventually I realized it was the priest's fear and ignorance that spoke to me, not God's voice, and that he was a human and therefore fallible. I felt compassion for his fearful state and saddened by his rigidity. And I was able to laugh at his pastoral listening and counseling skills – they sucked.

Being in touch with my spirit restored my respect for myself, cushioned my "fall" from the church, and helped me see past one man so that when I was ready I could regain the rituals of comfort and the tradition of community that the church offers.

This experience showed me that angels can protect us from psychological or emotional harm; but sometimes we need protection from physical perils too. I have an adventurous streak and I love to travel, two traits that have given them plenty of opportunities to watch over me.

After college I gave myself the gift of a trip to the Grand Canyon. I met up with a group who planned to descend the canyon in late morning and I excitedly joined them. Hiking down the Bright Angel Trail was spectacular and taxing in the early June sun. The weather is extremely unpredictable at the canyon: one minute it is a blazing 100 degrees while the next, hail the size of golf balls is falling from the sky.

Twenty minutes into the hike, I felt rumblings in my stomach that quickly turned into pain. I knew I couldn't continue and severely disappointed, I returned to my cabin and rested for the remainder of the day.

That evening there was a buzz of activity on the rim. I learned that one of the other hikers had fallen from the trail and been badly injured. She was airlifted to a trauma center. Hearing this, I felt a tremble inside and realized it could have been me. I prayed for her and prayed gratitude for my own safety.

The second day, a friend and I hopped on the canyon mules for a ride down to the Colorado River. The mules are bred for this type of journey (and I swear they have a sense of humor to boot). On the way down, the right side of the trail is cliff, rock, and canyon formation, while the left side is a drop straight down – very, very far down.

The mules love to walk on the outside edge and when they walk, of course, only two of their hooves are on the ground at any given time. And one of those two hooves is on sand that was crumbling beneath their immense weight. It feels like they're going to slide over the edge or the edge will crumble from their weight, sending mule and rider plummeting to the canyon floor.

By the time we safely reached the Colorado River, I was tense to say the least. It was hot but beautiful. I looked up to the top of the Canyon and thought, *the trip up must surely be easier and safer than the trip down.* Was I ever wrong.

After lunch we began our ascent under gorgeous blue skies. The trail leader came first, then me on "Miss Jane," followed by my friend and fifteen others. The expansiveness of the canyon was mesmerizing; my spirit felt like it was soaring without restraint. I was drinking in the other worldliness of the Canyon when I got a premonition of danger.

I snapped back to the reality that while beautiful, the canyon could also be deadly. I scanned ahead to the switchbacks leading to the rim. There were hikers ascending, people taking pictures, and our group riding mules. Everything looked fine. I relaxed in my saddle but the prickly feeling persisted.

Suddenly, I heard our leader's radio blaring a flash flood warning. Just as I was pondering how cloudless skies could cause flash floods, rain exploded overhead.

Worried, our guide hollered back at us, "Get a move on, and keep your mules nose-to-tail!" He had to get us out of the canyon before the heavy rain caused mudslides.

We pulled our rain parkas over our heads and huddled tightly onto the mules. They plodded along fairly quickly but had to be rested every so often. Our guide's nervous face only heightened our anxiety.

The wind picked up and began to howl past our hoods, while the rain blinded us to all but the four feet of trail immediately ahead. I prayed for a host of angels to protect us, but…I heard it just before I saw it: a deep rumbling followed by a flash as blue as the sky.

I heard the word "Stop!" in my mind and halted my mule, which stopped everyone behind me. The leader turned around and screamed, "Get Miss Jane moving, NOW!" But I was rooted to the spot. I couldn't move. As he began to turn his mule around to come back and grab my reins, I screamed, "Watch out!"

In that instant, a huge boulder came crashing in front of us, barely a foot ahead of him. The mules shied, and the situation almost unraveled as the realization that our guide had nearly been swept away by a crashing boulder dawned on each of us.

Shaken but determined to get to the top, we pushed our mules upward as the flash flooding began. We had just reached the ridge when the sky opened with thunder, lightening, and huge hailstones. Fifteen minutes later, the storm was gone and the blue sky had returned.

The leader asked me what had made me stop and call out to him. I told him. He looked deeply into my eyes and said, "Thank you…you saved my life." He had not heard the rumbling and never saw the boulder coming. I later learned that the flash of blue I had seen was a young woman in a blue parka who had been swept over the cliff by that same boulder. She had died almost instantly.

Twice I had been protected on the trail, and twice people were hurt. I had a choice: I could wonder, *why them and not me?* Or I could spend my time in gratitude, and follow the guidance given me by my angels and share this story with you.

It's your choice whether to make something positive out of cruel circumstances. I often think of the good done by John Walsh, creator and host of "America's Most Wanted" and primary mover behind the founding of the National Center for Missing & Exploited Children. His work on behalf of missing children began after his own six year old son, Adam, was kidnapped from a shopping mall and found murdered sixteen days later.

I don't believe that God or the angels choose who will die and who will be saved. We live in a world in motion where human misery and tragedy is largely the result of man's actions and choices. But we do have access to help from beyond our human perspective.

This doesn't mean everyone will survive terrible car crashes or diseases. It doesn't mean that bad things won't happen to our children or us. However, it does mean there is help available to us, if we are open and ask for it.

Touched by an angel

Many times our helpers comfort and heal us in ways different from what we expect. We might pray for one thing and receive something totally different. This is the time to let go of control and trust the spiritual help so readily available. When we are open to the help in all its forms, we discover that God can make us smile in even the darkest of times.

After finally listening to my guidance to leave my beloved job in the E.R. and use my intuitive gifts full-time, I moved from New York to California.

But my leap of faith got me no parades nor an answer to, "What's next?" How was I supposed to get started? How was I going to support myself? I thought that having followed my guidance, I deserved some specific answers from God or my angels. When no answers were forthcoming, I began to second guess my decision to quit my job.

One afternoon I went down to the beach to ponder the empty silence that had replaced my once resounding guidance. I felt alone, out on a limb, and without the angelic comfort I needed. When I arrived at the beach, I was annoyed to find hordes of people milling around. I was feeling alone and I wanted to be alone.

Looking south, I spotted a quiet, empty stretch about 250 yards away, and made my way there. As I headed toward this sanctuary, I silently dared anyone to stop me. I was feeling more than a little surly about all the people impinging on my solitude.

Fortunately, my inner turmoil was bigger than my pride, so as I walked, I prayed for God to send comfort to me. I needed to be reminded that I was on the right path. I settled down on the sand, sat back, relaxed, and watched the soothing rise and fall of the waves – until a man walked up and squarely blocked my view. Anger spurted through me. I was about to shoo him away when he spoke.

"What do you think you're doing?" he demanded. "You can't be here." His attitude was defiant and I was in no mood for dealing with a pain in the ass.

"It's the only place around here without people," I answered.

He looked at me strangely. "How did you get here?" Then he added, "You can't stay."

I was in no mood for silly questions or to be told I couldn't sit on a free beach. I was about to issue a less than friendly retort, when I suddenly noticed there were eight or ten people standing on the sand nearby. Guards surrounded them and a barricade held back the hordes of people I'd seen earlier. Then a woman walked past and gave me a smile.

I was filled with joy as I recognized her and waved back. Then I took in the whole of my situation and began to laugh. My prayer had been answered. I had somehow gotten past the security guards and parked myself smack in the middle of the filming of an episode of "Touched by an Angel." And the comforting smile I received had come, of course, from "Monica," one of the show's two angels.

**Don't forget your sense of humor
when you get rescued from yourself!**

Rats in the pyramid

We don't usually laugh when thinking about death. As a youngster I had a great fear of death, which increased dramatically after I went to see "Night of the Living Dead." You'd never find me in a graveyard at night. Show me a coffin and the hair stood up on my arms. Even though I swore off horror films early on, my fear of the unknown lingered and deepened, thanks to my rampant imagination.

None of this was on my mind, however, when I was traveling in Egypt with a friend. One night we decided to see the sarcophagus at the top of the Great Pyramid of Giza, one of the original Seven Wonders of the World. We had been forewarned that at midnight, the lights inside the pyramid would go out for thirty minutes, and so we planned to be back outside before that.

Having made it to the top and seen the amazing King's Burial Chamber with its huge red granite sarcophagus, we started back down the passageway. The corridor was rugged and lacked the safety rails or helpful signs found in American tourist attractions. At least it was decently lit.

Wrong. The tomb keeper's watch must have been fast because suddenly we were plunged into total blackness and silence. Only a little daunted, we continued our precarious descent guided by feel alone. Inching our way along the many twists and turns, we held hands, duck waddling under the low earthen roof.

I literally couldn't see my hand in front of my face. I asked God to send a few angels to guide us safely to the exit. I remembered from our trip up that there was a very dangerous section where the path turned sharply to avoid a drop of about thirty feet, but I had no idea how close to it we were.

Making our way in pitch-black darkness was both tedious and nerve-wracking – until suddenly I realized where I was and began to laugh. The echoes of my laughter off the stone walls only made me laugh more. My friend thought I had lost my mind.

"Christel," she whispered, "are you okay?"

At this point tears were streaming down my face, and the more I tried to speak, the louder I howled.

"It's okay," she soothed, "We'll get out. You'll be okay."

I only laughed harder and sputtered, "I'm okay!"

"You are?"

"Yes," I managed. I took a few breaths, and between smothered giggles and howls, I said, "What's the thing I am most terrified of?"

Without hesitation she replied, "Coffins and graveyards."

"And where are we now?"

"In the largest Giza pyrami…" Then she burst into laughter, too, which set me off again.

"We are in the world's largest graveyard, in complete darkness, with an ancient and spooky coffin upstairs! It could only happen to you. How do you feel?"

"Fantastic, other than the fact that now I have to go to the bathroom badly, plus we are on a very dangerous section in the pitch dark," I replied, my sides aching from laughing so hard.

We continued our way down even more slowly as our giggling made the route twice as treacherous. Suddenly I had a very strong intuition to stop. In fact, I could not have moved if I wanted to. My legs felt like lead and my body sank down into the dirt. This otherworldly feeling was not foreign to me – I had experienced it a few times before. I grabbed my friend's hand.

"Let's wait here until the lights come back on."

So she sat down next to me, and we dangled our feet over the ledge we were on. Our hands were scraped and bruised, our clothes dusty and dirty. Then we heard a movement in the dark.

"Rats," I whispered. We froze. Suddenly nothing was funny anymore.

Then we noticed a small light moving toward us. A tomb guard had heard our screams of laughter and thought we were in trouble. So he used the only light available to look for us: a tiny Bic lighter. He found us clinging to each other, white-faced and stock-still.

He was terribly proud to have rescued us and bragged to the other guards when we got back outside. He was a hero, so we didn't explain that our hysteria was laughter, not fear.

When the lights came back on, I realized I had left my jacket on the ledge. When I went back in to retrieve it, I was able to see where we had been sitting. We had taken a wrong turn – the flimsy cord that served as a guardrail was missing and we were one step away from falling headfirst into an empty shaft thirty feet deep.

I prayed gratitude that night for my friend, my guardian angel, my ability to laugh at myself, the absence of rats, and our safety – but most of all for God's sense of humor, which was not lost on me.

Has reading these accounts of grace in action made you more aware of the possibilities that await you?

Are you ready to tap into your intuition and receive all the divine help you could possibly want?

Do you remember the simple yet important information you need to begin your journey?

You can open the lines of communication to God by expressing gratitude daily. It will also raise your vibration and make you a healing force on our planet.

You can ask for help anytime, anywhere and it doesn't cost you a thing, but your request for intuition, guidance, or help must be sincere, and it's important to refrain from setting any conditions on what kind of help it must be. It will surely limit the response.

Pay attention. Listen and watch carefully for a response (especially on trains), and be aware of the resonance of truth when you are connecting with your spirit. Last but not least:

- Not liking your guidance won't change it.
- If you hear nothing and you have been sincere, ask if this is your time to rest, pray, and wait.
- Asking for a sign to confirm your intuition is smart, not a sign of weakness.

- Accept that even prayer cannot save all lives.

When you recognize that you have received guidance whether it was through an event that occurred, a voice that spoke in your head, the intervention of a stranger, or a message in a dream – say thank you.

Consider the possibility that your guidance may save a life; get over your discomfort and share the information you've been given and take the action you've been told to take.
Stay true to what you know...

Chapter Seven

POSITIVE ENERGY IS CONTAGIOUS

Living intuitively by paying attention to our spiritual helpers can have a wonderful effect on us, not just because they help us when we ask for help, but because their positive energy raises our own energy. As they say, we are known by the company we keep.

When I say "positive energy," I am talking about the actual electromagnetic energy that we, like all living things, emit. This energy, which is present in every cell in our body, radiates from us in the form of vibrations. When the frequency of your vibration is high, you have "positive energy."

So, although we are all beings of flesh and blood, we are much more than that. We are beings of light and energy, and we all run at a particular vibration – some people much higher or lower than others.

High vibration is synonymous with health, happiness, love, joy, and passion. A low vibration is synonymous with illness, hatred, resentment, revenge, and jealousy.

We all make choices daily – consciously and unconsciously – that either raise or lower our vibration. People who live with divine direction choose more easily

89

to forgive and feel compassion which is a high vibration, while those who choose to be narrow-minded and spiteful have a much lower vibration. Also, associating with low-vibration people or being in an abusive relationship can and will lower your vibration.

Living intuitively raises your vibration because being in the flow with less distraction frees us to be our true selves - forgiving, compassionate, and loving. Sharing that high vibration is healing to those around you.

Have you ever noticed how you respond to happy people who are smiling? You feel good around them and tend to be uplifted into their happiness. What about when you are around a playful person, don't you feel more playful, light, and fun?

Now compare that with being around a forgiving person – you've seen them on talk shows or perhaps are lucky enough to know one personally – where a mother forgives someone for driving drunk and killing her child. Are you not in awe, is not your compassion, and desire to forgive awakened to some degree?

Positive high vibration energy is contagious. When you are around a profound role model, you can't help but want to strive to be a better person and emulate the qualities of that person.

Living a divinely directed life compels you to rise above petty jealousies and feuds, and to replace resentment with forgiveness.

Raise your vibration

As you may recall I have been clairvoyant since age eight and read souls for a living. Able to see a running "video" of your childhood at lightning speed, I see the traumas you have endured, your personal beliefs, your level of self-esteem, and more. I also see your secrets.

One of the most common secrets I find is that you haven't forgiven yourself for a past mistake or decision you made, and thus don't deserve to ask for help or live an easier life.

Another serious secret that I find is that you actually take pride in struggling with your problems and overcoming adversity on your own. During an intuitive reading, whether private or in a workshop, such misplaced pride is revealed. I say misplaced because struggling, unless you enjoy such suffering, is a waste of your valuable energy, and does nothing to build your worth as a person.

Do you secretly like to struggle? If so, it's like not asking for directions and driving around lost for days and days. If you're on your way to visit a new friend, it's just a silly waste of time, but if you're on your way to the emergency room, it's tragic.

Do you really believe that struggling builds character, and if so, what exactly are you planning to do with all this character? The truth is you are only creating a low vibration lifestyle. What's more, you will receive no brownie points either here or in the sweet hereafter for your fortitude in overcoming adversity. The badge of honor you wear so proudly doesn't go with you when you cross over.

I have been privileged to accompany a number of people on their journey to the afterlife, and I can tell you from my firsthand knowledge that there is no special section for those who have managed to get through life without any help.

There's only one big "room" up there and it's filled with an assortment of eclectic beings, all bathed in the softest white light, all of whom chose the light over the darkness. It is the most loving and safe place you will ever know. There is no struggle, pain, or disease. There is only unconditional love, joy, and the freedom to be loved. It is at the threshold to the "room" where you can choose to enter the light.

The good news is that you don't need to wait for your death to live in that high vibration. Communicating with your spirit through your intuition reminds you who you really are. The light is around you all the time and can bring the solace of knowing that you are not ever alone.

I want you to change your ideas about asking for help so you can live a divinely inspired life, which is so much easier and more fulfilling. This is how you raise your vibration and help me bring our planet to the tipping point of positivity.

Yes, I know you have invested a lot of time and energy believing you don't deserve help, and I know you don't like being wrong, but if you could set those concepts aside momentarily, I have a surprise for you: life doesn't have to be as hard as you are making it.

No matter what your need, whether it's an answer to a straightforward question, a solution to a serious problem, or something as simple as finding Maple Street, you can get it just for the asking.

There is nothing standing between you and a divinely directed life with a wealth of assistance. Nothing that is, except some old ideas. They may feel too big or too deep, or like they would require long term therapy or inner growth work to change. Again, that's just another outdated belief, and you can change it now.

Here are seven simple steps to get you started:

1. Write down on a piece of paper why you think you are ineligible to receive easy guidance, or why you simply don't ask for help.

2. Fold the paper and on the outside of it write: *I am now suspending these beliefs and requirements for receiving help.*

3. Burn the paper while saying the following prayer: *Please transmute my old ideas to new, high vibration, and positive expectations of divine help.*

4. Be courageous, take a risk, and ask sincerely for help with something that is troubling you right now. You can ask for comfort, peace, direction, inspiration, or anything else you need. Write this request down in a journal.

5. Dismiss any negative thinking from your mind, by writing down and repeating this phrase: *I like it when I find easy solutions to my problems, and I give myself permission to do so now.* Keep your thoughts in a high vibration and a state of positive anticipation.

6. Express gratitude for the forthcoming answers and solutions: *Thank you for helping me and making my life easier. I am grateful for my willingness and ability to change easily and be in the flow.*

7. Be attentive for the next 48 hours for synchronistic events, new ideas, a change in attitude, or unexpected solutions. Write them down in your journal.

Let's return to the irrefutable fact that divine guidance is always available and all you have to do is ask for it. So what is stopping you from seeking help? Answer me this: do you ask for God's help when your life isn't going well? Do you ask for help when you need an answer to a question? Do you ask for help when you are depressed or sad, or feel like you are bending under the weight of your life? If not, *why?*

Now imagine you are stuck in quicksand and are slowly sinking beneath the surface. Would you ask for help? Of course you would. You know that if you don't, you will sink deeper and deeper until you suffocate and die. I bet you'd shout for help at the top of your lungs! But what if I told you that you were sinking closer and closer to suffocation every time you refuse to ask for guidance?

Without help, you are expending needless energy struggling to overcome the problems in your life. And just like struggling to get out of quicksand, all that happens is you use up your energy, sink even faster, and eventually lose the battle anyway.

What I am trying to tell you is that the quality of your life is on the line – you can choose to make your life painful and difficult, or joyous and flowing. You can choose to live with guidance, or you can choose to die without it.

When I used the analogy of the quicksand, it was easy for you to see the seriousness of the situation: if you think you will die, you won't hesitate to ask for help. But asking for intuitive help becomes more complicated if you don't recognize you are dying. Subtle, life-draining situations as opposed to life-threatening situations arise all the time in your life.

And because you don't realize the real danger in tolerating such situations, you put off asking for help, or you debate whether you ought to ask, or you take time to worry whether you deserve it.

This debating costs you dearly; your choice to struggle through life without help, or quietly endure your grief, sadness, and overwhelm, is draining your energy, affecting your daily health and happiness, and causing long-term damage to your physical, emotional, and spiritual well-being.

It's every bit as important to treat these energy draining patterns as it is a physical illness. Ask for comfort to relieve your anxiety, ask for creative ways to alleviate your financial stress, inspiration to find quality time to take care of yourself, and encouragement when your hope is fading. Don't live your life alone.

Can you see your light?

We are beings of light and must work diligently to be otherwise. I see so much needless struggle and suffering in this world, and as a medical intuitive, I see the harm it wreaks on your heart, body, and mind – and eventually on your soul. I see the amount of light emanating from your soul.

When you were a child, before you were hurt and learned to believe bad things about yourself, or learned that struggle builds character, your child soul thrummed with vitality, love and light.

I've delivered babies and reveled in that first glimpse of light that is familiar, loving, and exciting to me. But just as my view of that "room" gradually fades from me as I fall back to earth and return to physical form, my first glimpse of your shining soul fades from my view, as you begin to separate from your spiritual nature.

The joy and love that were once so bright have been replaced by negativity, judgment, fear, anger, guilt, and low self-esteem. Your life experiences dim your soul with a shadowy film as you learn prejudice or harbor vengeance.

Other choices you make as an adult such as dabbling with dark influences that feed your ego, telling you that you are right and others are wrong, can also play a major role in dimming the light of your soul and separating you from the divine.

I've seen people so removed from their true essence that the soul has been completely blotted out by the darkness. These people have clung to low vibration choices, and sometimes have even traded their light for fame, wealth, power, and pride in being right.

They are shrouded in an illusion that they are "special" and emanate no discernable vibration. When I am around them, it feels like there is an impenetrable wall between them and me. I now know that I am being protected from their influence and vibration.

One man I worked with had to be right even though his arrogance almost killed his wife. To this day he refuses to take responsibility for his negativity, victim attitude, and need for sympathy; he continues to blame others for his woes, and takes comfort in being right, as the darkness soothes his ego, seducing him farther away from his spirit.

This unwillingness and rigidity takes tremendous effort. Such a waste of energy is sad, but the real problem is his lack of conflict with his choices; he still works diligently to prove how right he is. His great distance from the light disconnects him from his conscience, and prevents him from being spiritually responsible. He refuses to explore a different paradigm from the one he stubbornly clings to, so I refused to work with him any further.

I long to see you reconnect with your your soul; it has allowed people to heal from incurable diseases and brought an inner peace to those suffering from tremendous feelings of inadequacy. It has healed victims of abuse and given courage to those who lived in fear.

You must first let go of your belief that you are bad or deserve to be punished, or that help is not available to you because you are flawed and therefore different from those who are able to receive help.

Open up to the possibility that you can make high vibration choices now because the light will always welcome you back. Your soul is the part of you that recognizes truth, burns with inspiration and kindness, and revels in forgiveness and compassion. Your soul is the part of you that is most like the divine.

Help is available to you here and now if you only ask. Or do you prefer to be "special?"

When you regularly tap into your guidance, you will effortlessly make better choices that make you happy and healthy, because you are operating at a higher vibration and in tune with your spiritual nature.

When your vibration increases, you sometimes find yourself saying something kind to a complete stranger for no apparent reason. Other times you feel very comfortable with who you are. You have more self-esteem and more courage. You laugh more. Pain lessens and despair lifts. There is a natural desire to be of service that overshadows fears or doubts.

Doing a reading on someone with a high vibration is always a delight for me. Aside from the pure pleasure of being around someone like that, the colors I see in their energy field are more exciting than a Fourth of July fireworks display.

There is a 3D quality and an almost explosive and tangible joy that infuses my heart and causes a tingling of fun and smiles inside of me; reading someone with a very low vibration is not nearly the same.

I read Jan, a woman in her early sixties, who had spent her entire life feeling inferior to others. She came to see me because she was slightly depressed and felt a general malaise about the world. I found no significant physical problems, but her emotions were shut down, and her connection to God was completely cut off.

Her crown chakra[1], which is the conduit for our connection to the divine, was completely closed, and she was without inspiration or guidance. Early on it feels lonely, sometimes frightening, and empty inside from being separated from your true nature.

The priority task for Jan was to open up her crown chakra and reconnect to her Higher Power. Without reconnection, her soul would not thrive and she would continue to become more depressed, more desolate, and more convinced that she was defective.

She would drift away into an apathetic place where she would go through the motions of life without any real feeling, without any real passion, and without any real connection to God, to others, or to herself.

The quickest way to reconnect is to pray gratitude. I took Jan's hand so we could pray gratitude for all the wondrous things in her life. She looked at me as though I had two heads – her life sure didn't feel wondrous, but she took my hand anyway.

I began to give thanks for Jan's health, for her ability to appreciate the joy and beauty in life, for the people she had in her life, and for the longevity of her life. I prayed gratitude for the incredible day that we were experiencing.

---

[1] Chakras: spiritual energy centers in the body.

I thanked God for Jan's ability to reach out for help, for her courage to come to me and try to resolve her problem, for her awareness that there was a problem, and for her willingness to do whatever was needed to heal her spiritual issue.

Shortly into our prayers, Jan began to weep as she started to let the divine into her heart. Slowly she began to realize that she didn't have to do anything to deserve God's love, that it was hers by virtue of just being alive in that moment.

Jan saw that she was worthy of God's love. And in that moment, as I held her hand, Jan felt the power, the majesty, and the love of God. She felt herself opening up and surrendering to a power higher than herself. In that moment, Jan received grace and it changed her life forever.

I gave her "homework" to pray gratitude daily, keep her heart open, and reconnect with God. The lines of communication had been reconnected. Now she was ready to pray for guidance. And now she would get it.

Don't sit in your house waiting for God to call back if your telephone is out of order.

Chapter Eight

THE SECRET TO SPIRITUALITY

Living at a high vibration is the secret habit you need to become a spiritual person. Raise your vibration by seeking out high vibration people, and doing things that make you feel safe, and jazz you such as praying, lighting candles, singing, dancing, laughing, or playing with a pet.

If you choose to be compassionate or forgiving by letting go of your past hurts and living in the present, your vibration will continue to rise. Should you associate with loving, tender, good-humored, and gentle souls, and resonate with their vibration, your vibration will begin to soar.

Spiritual growth requires looking at your shadow, the buried and unconscious part of yourself that drives your behavior, lowers your vibration, and prevents you from achieving your dreams. Such knowledge is powerful and while you may not like everything you see, you always have the choice to change it.

No matter how bad your situation, you are never without the option to raise your vibration. Asking for guidance is a choice available to you at every moment, and opening your heart to the loving presence of the divine can quickly comfort you.

When you take actions and make choices that raise your vibration, you will learn to reconnect with your spirit, giving you access to more of your innate abilities including your intuition. Your divine knowledge will help you become the person you are meant to be, by opening you to more possibilities for growth.

Spiritual growth happens every day we choose to be spiritually responsible: making the choice to change whatever is not working in your life, including parts of yourself.

This means that you take responsibility for the current state of your life, for your choices, and for their consequences, no matter what illness, wounds, or problems you have and no matter who or what caused them. You do this by living in the moment, being honest about what you want, and choosing not to be a powerless victim.

Accepting spiritual responsibility means realizing that there are no mysteries as to why your life is the way it is. You will understand that making choices that help you raise your vibration, help put you in the flow.

Conversely, you won't be mystified or wonder why your supposed positive thoughts aren't producing positive effects. You'll know that secretly you are harboring victim, vengeful, martyr, or injured child energies that keep you in a low vibration and emotional limitation.

Does this sound like a hard path to take? You might be surprised to hear that people have told me that when they took spiritual responsibility for their lives, they breathed easier. It was like having a weight removed from their shoulders. All of a sudden, they were no longer at the mercy of others or their past. They didn't need someone else to change in order to be happy. They were truly the captain of their own ship.

Soon you will yearn for more than just growth; you'll aim for true spiritual evolution.

Spiritual evolution in your lifetime

Spiritual evolution is what you do over the course of your life, how you treat others, help your fellow man, and learn to forgive easily. It's the process of listening to your soul and making choices that bring you to a higher vibration.

Your ability to hear your soul's desires and make such choices is dependent upon your healing the three major issues that need to be worked through and resolved: learning to feel safe, letting go of the desire to have power over others, and living life courageously and confidently.

These issues, which correspond to the first three chakras, are further complicated by erroneous beliefs that cause you to make unconscious choices that are not always in your highest good, leaving your chakras undeveloped.

When you don't feel safe, for example, it can be hard to open your heart to the spiritual world, because living your life according to your intuition may conflict with your tribal rules. Although belonging to a tribe can make you feel safe, it has to be a tribe supportive of your choices. Otherwise, like my incident with the priest, you may be kicked out of a tribe because your way is different from theirs.

If your tribe says that asking for help is a sign of a weak person, or listening for intuition is just too woo-woo, you may have a conflict on your hands: do you listen to the people who taught you about the world, or listen to your spirit?

Tribal beliefs are rules about life taught to you by your family, teachers, and religious institutions. The people in these groups make up your various "tribes." The purpose of a tribe is to protect you, educate you, and raise you to adulthood so that you can become a useful member of it. The purpose of tribal beliefs is to bind the group together through a common belief system. This is not a bad thing per se, unless what you want is at odds with what your tribe has taught you.

If you have a conflict about wanting more in life, whether it's an intuition filled life, or love, it will be difficult for these good things to come your way. If your limiting tribal belief states *you only get one true love in life,* and your relationship has ended, asking for a new love in your life will create inner turmoil until you change the belief, or give up wanting another love.

Spiritual evolution requires you to take a risk and step away from the tribe and hear the voice of your spirit. It demands that you be authentic, honest, and face your shadow to remove any low vibration thoughts, actions, or beliefs such as "I don't deserve happiness."

Ignoring the voice of your spirit will betray you because it will keep you out of the flow and from finding your purpose and passion in life. You, however, will think it is the spiritual world that has betrayed you. Therefore:

- Don't ask for help to be happy if you have an unconscious belief that being too happy is selfish, or that it's not okay to be happy if people you love aren't also happy.

- Don't ask for guidance for a better life unless you are clear that it's okay to want a better life, or have more than you now have.

- Don't ask for a longer life if you're not excited about the life you're living right now.

Low vibration rules and beliefs are misguided or just plain erroneous. They wouldn't necessarily be a big problem if you knew they were just beliefs. The trouble is, they are treated like facts, so you think they are true. Here are some beliefs that you may think are facts:

- My problems are small, and it's not right to ask for help when there are people worse off than me, people who really need the help.

- Asking for help means I'm weak.

- If I ask for help and get it, I will owe something, and I don't like the feeling of owing something.

- If I struggle through on my own, it builds character.

Your spiritual path can become complicated with too many low vibration ideas. Take the time to explore your belief system, and let me start you off with some alternative ideas:

- Your receiving guidance does not deprive anyone else of it. God is never going to run out of time or energy to help you.

- Asking for help usually means you are smart enough to know when you need it. And smart enough to know that if you struggle through on your own, you'll only get exhausted. If you doubt it, look up the definition of "struggle."

- Guidance doesn't come with a price tag. When your angels help you, you don't owe them a thing (except to say thank you).

Please see my book *Sacred Choices* to help you on this journey to teach you how to identify and quickly change your thoughts to a high and limitless vibration and take you out of your conflict.

Limiting thoughts about the spiritual realm can be much subtler than the examples I gave you earlier. They come in the guise of religious instruction and it's a rare child who doesn't swallow them hook, line, and sinker. Here are some of the "facts" my clients were taught:

Mary: "My tribe taught me that only spiritual people can communicate with angels. Spiritual people were not ordinary people like us; therefore angels were beyond our reach."

Natalie: "Angels are sacred, like saints, and should not be bothered for mundane, earthly matters. It would be almost sacrilegious to call for help from such a spiritual being."

Will: "Angels only guard little children, and once you grow up you are on your own."

These "facts" are not only wrong, but they stand in the way of receiving an enormous amount of help in the form of guidance, inspiration, comfort, and angelic intervention.

If you put limitations on the spiritual world it will severely slow or limit your spiritual evolution.

**Your evolution slows to a crawl
when the needs of your ego, or need to be right
makes you deaf to the voice of your spirit.**

Pack for your spiritual journey

You are on your spiritual path this very moment and should bring some essential items like an open mind, courage, and a willingness to embrace your true nature.

Make high vibration choices to make your journey more enjoyable. You can choose to simply pray for the world each day, step out of a powerless victim state, or listen to the guidance that is shouting from the depths of your soul.

But please don't weigh yourself down with things that will slow your journey, and at times make it difficult. Let go of your excess baggage and:

- Set down your pride.
- Set down your need to be right.

- Set down your badge of honor for working hard.

Don't let your pride and the idea that you have to do it all on your own, close your heart to help.

The downfall of man has always been caused by pride. This is true whether that downfall be one's health, relationship, finances, or professional success. Taken to its extreme, pride is the cause of blood feuds. It is the fuel for revenge, hatred, jealousy, suffering, and denial.

Talking about pride is tricky. Some people have told me that pride means thinking too well of yourself or acknowledging your ability to play the piano skillfully. Pride is akin to boasting, they say.

I worked with a woman who has struggled most of her life. Nancy was a single parent with a high-stress job and few friends. She wasn't very happy. But suggesting to her that she could ask for help and her life could be easier was no easy task. She sputtered in anger that her life couldn't be easier because of her past "mistakes." She didn't really deserve an easier life. (You can probably recognize this by now as a tribal belief.)

Nancy needed to be right, so she clung to her convictions. However, the truth was, her life could be easier and her "mistakes" did not bar her from God's help.

I gave her a few seconds to bask in her excuses, then said, "What if I tell you not only how you have contributed – quite generously – to your life being difficult, but why you won't consider changing it." That got her attention.

"You don't want an easy life. You wear your struggle like a badge of honor. You take great pride in your fortitude, your ability to keep going no matter the odds against you. You are proud of the way you persevere in the face of adversity. If I took that adversity away, you would feel like a nobody."

I have to give Nancy credit. She had the smarts and good grace not to explode in angry defenses and rationalizations about her life. She looked me squarely in the eye and said, "You're right I won't ask anyone for help, not my family or God or spiritual guides. If life were easy..."

Her voice trailed off as she realized that deep down she was in a huge conflict. She hated struggling in life but was afraid if she didn't struggle and overcome, she would not only have no self-esteem, but she wouldn't be able to be forgiven and pay for her "mistake" of getting pregnant out of wedlock.

Nancy's pride in punishing herself and living in struggle had become more important than anything else in her life. Her pride in her agenda had blotted out God's love, and her stubbornness had contributed to a low vibration in her corner of the world. She dug in her heels, wore her struggles like a badge of honor, and ceased to grow spiritually or change any aspect of her life even though she was clearly conscious of having a choice to live differently.

Her low vibration eventually drove away all of the people in her life. Sadly, as she nears the twilight of her life, she still refuses to accept God's love or her inherent gifts and talents, and is still paying dearly for her earlier "mistake." She blames God for abandoning her, even though it is her pride in being right that has ruined her life. Until Nancy becomes willing to let go of the need to be right, there is no healing possible for her.

Pride comes in many forms, even in ways that appear laudable. One of my clients told me he takes great pride in working hard for his family. Sounds good, doesn't it? The problem was, it was all about his agenda and needs.

John worked hard all the time – on workdays, days off, during his free time. He worked hard whether he felt good, bad, or downright sick. He worked when he was in pain. In fact, he worked even harder when he was in pain. He never took a day off.

John considered this honorable. He took pride in the fact that he could keep working against all odds. The badge of honor John wore may have been invisible, but it was so huge, he actually walked tilted to one side.

If John's ability to persevere against all odds were taken away, he would consider himself a failure as a husband, father, and man. He attached his self-worth to his ability to struggle through adversity and wake up the next day to do it all over again.

What I saw was a man slavishly attached to his tribal beliefs, a man willing to die for his convictions. Sadly, John refused to consider that he was being prideful in an unhealthy way and worked himself into an early grave.

There is a strong reason why I say that pride is always the cause of a person's downfall. Holding on to your erroneous tribal beliefs can ruin your life. Because you cannot entertain other possibilities, you remain locked in a low vibration, destined to keep wearing that exhausting badge of honor. It is more important for you to be "right" than happy, healthy, or even alive, and needing to be right can actually kill you.

You don't want to carry such heavy baggage with your through life. Instead, when you pack for your spiritual journey, bring a good attitude, a high vibration, a willingness to change quickly, and your intuition. Your luggage will be so light, you'll forget you've even brought it with you!

Pride is digging in your heels, closing your mind,
and refusing to know anything
but what you already know.

Bring the real you

Own who you really are, a spiritual being in the process of learning and growing. Take a risk now and again, and try to live your life in a different way.

I worked with a woman named Ginger, who is quite a painter. Yet, when I remarked on her talent, she brushed me aside. "I'm okay," she replied. "There are others much better. Now da Vinci, he was a real painter."

Ginger's need to be right in her assessment of her talents actually prevented her from rating them highly enough, which got in the way of her success and satisfaction in life.

Nancy, John, and Ginger are classic examples of people whose self-esteem comes from the outside, not the inside. When you have no self-esteem, you must garner praise and accolades from others to feel good about yourself. You are dependent on your boss's approval, a critic's opinions, your spouse's smile, and your friend's remarks.

Unfortunately, even if you win such accolades, your self-esteem can be taken away the moment anyone says something critical. When one art critic said Ginger's painting was great, she had a short-lived high...until another critic said it stunk. She was like a tiny rag doll buffeted by the ever-changing winds.

Acknowledging your gifts and talents fills you with confidence. It allows you to own your personal power and not give it away to others. When you know you are an ethical person and someone calls you unethical, you don't fall apart. Your strength is inside - you know your worth. You develop self-esteem by:

- Making commitments to yourself that you keep.

- Valuing your personal code of honor.

- Owning your gifts and talents and letting go of false humility - if you are good, own it!

- Not looking for attention or validation from others - give it to yourself.

You are honoring yourself, God, and others when you own your talents, such as:

- The ability to create a warm and safe home.

- The knack of remembering important dates in people's lives.

- The ability to light up a room just by walking in it.

- Being funny.

- The ability to stay neutral and see both sides of an argument without prejudice.

- The ability to entertain by weaving a good story.

Think of it this way: When you fill out a resume, do you neglect to mention your abilities or talents in your field? If you did, wouldn't it dishonor all the people who taught, mentored, or otherwise helped you learn and grow professionally over the years? Besides, what employer would want to hire you?

Owning all of your talents – in every field – builds your self-esteem and frees you from the need to look to others to feel good about yourself. It keeps you from being stuck in pride that comes from low vibration activities, such as struggling on your own.

I have a client who I think is simply amazing. He is funny and warm, a bright light on the planet. Yet he has low self-esteem and little confidence or courage in certain areas. Put him in a business arena and he can outdo Donald Trump. But put him in a relationship, and his fire goes out. When I asked him to tell me why he was amazing, he was quite taken aback at first.

"I never thought of myself as amazing," he mused.

"Well, I do," I countered. "So out with it."

All he could find to say was that he had a good business mind, and perhaps that was mildly amazing.

I looked at him and tried a different approach.

"Tell me who you are, what qualities you have, how someone would describe you." He said he was kind, compassionate, and funny.

"That's a great start," I said. "Now tell me what makes you who you are. What is it about you that you can always count on? For example, in times of stress are you the one who keeps his sense of humor and doesn't lose his cool?" I already knew this was true, but I waited for him to nod in agreement.

"And are you a good listener to your friends?" He nodded again. I felt like a dentist extracting teeth, but eventually I pulled a list of his qualities from him. He looked nonplussed as the list grew.

"How can you call being compassionate or being a good listener a talent or gift?" he protested. "We're supposed to be that way."

Here was a classic example of a hidden tribal belief being unveiled. I quickly scanned his energy and saw a picture of him sitting contentedly on his deck. I said,

"How about Andrea Bocelli? Do you think he is a talented singer?"

"Oh, yes," he replied, "I love to listen to him when I'm out on my deck. He's marvelous, so very talented."

"So, singing is a talent or gift, but being a good listener or leader is not?"

"Well...yes."

My client considered singing as a gift from God because he couldn't do it. The value of his own gifts and talents was negated because they were his. This is false humility, even if he is not conscious of it being so. The point is that he is certain he is right: Andrea Bocelli is gifted and he is not. We're back at pride.

Many people believe it is boastful to acknowledge their gifts and talents. Their family has taught them never to blow their own horn. I can't tell you how many clients have this tribal belief. Are you ready for the truth about this one? The false modesty of ignoring or downplaying your gifts and talents is a slap in God's face. You received a gift, yet will not own it.

But when you heal the part of you that feels unworthy, the part that doesn't value your own gifts and talents, your life will become unrecognizable.

When you become comfortable in your own skin, you will develop the courage to get out in the world and try something new – start a relationship, go on a safari in Africa, get out of a bad marriage, or trust your intuition when you are told to start a business. Taking these first steps takes you out of the mundane and can lead to a life of greatness, filled with joy, adventure, love, confidence, peacefulness, and passion.

No matter how bad your situation, you are never without the option to raise your vibration.

Chapter Nine

ARE YOU DESTINED FOR GREATNESS?

Nowadays, almost everyone I meet seems to be on a spiritual path or is searching for a purpose in life. It has become very popular. Unfortunately, many people have cluttered their search with religious baggage.

For example, there are those who believe that walking a spiritual path involves struggle or sacrifice, being alone in the world, or seeing all the difficult times in life as spiritual lessons necessary for their soul's evolution. Yet the truth is if you take responsibility for what you have created and make choices that are good for you, you don't need to learn so many tough lessons.

Some people search in exotic lands for a more spiritually evolved person to bestow wisdom upon them or reveal a grandiose, meaningful, or important purpose in their lives. Others seem to require adherence to rituals like meditation or vegetarianism to be spiritual. Yet, 99% of the people I have asked could not answer these questions:

- What is your purpose in life?
- How do you know when you have reached your goal and have become a spiritual person?

- And what happens then?

I have a proposal for you: What if your life purpose is to be a good mother, a good friend, a community net worker or simply to be happy? And what if being happy is a spiritual way of life?

When you are happy, your vibration is high, you hear God's voice, live in the flow, and have a positive impact on the world. Your happiness is easily spread to other people in your family, your community and around the world; could this be an important purpose? Imagine the possibilities!

Are you not drawn to and feel better around happy people? What if you are the one who has the courage to break with tribal ways and do what brings you joy? What if you are the one who shows others that following guidance makes life easy, light, and fun? Do you have any clue of the ripple effect you would have on the people you meet?

When you accept a leadership role in healing our world by raising your vibration and living your purpose, you are on the road to greatness.

A man named Francis said it best many years ago:

> "Where there is hatred, let me sow love...
> where there is despair, hope

> where there is darkness, light
> and where there is sadness, joy."

You make a difference in this world by contributing a high vibration of happiness, love, safety, forgiveness, truth, creativity, and joy into our world. Living in a high vibration and being happy is your true spiritual nature, and contributes immensely to the healing of the planet and brings you closer to God. It's a life of greatness.

Isn't that a spectacular calling?

Remember the reading I did for Jan, who had to open the lines of communication with God by praying gratitude before she was able to hear her guidance? Two days after our prayers together, she called me. She was both excited and scared.

Her guidance had told her to quit her job and retire, something she hadn't planned to do for another four years. She was excited because she no longer enjoyed her job, but she was scared because she wasn't sure if she could make it financially on her pension.

Then something else hit her. What would she do with the rest of her life? She prayed for more guidance, but heard nothing else. I encouraged her to follow her initial guidance. Everything would work out ten times better than it was at the moment.

Jan chose to trust her guidance and retire from work. She told me, however, that she still had heard nothing regarding her next step. We prayed together, and I heard Jan's guidance very clearly. It was this: "Relax and enjoy your life."

Jan was perplexed. "What kind of guidance is that?" she asked.

"Very clear guidance," I responded.

"How am I supposed to relax and enjoy my life?" she asked.

"First, you retired. Now you figure out what makes you happy. Then you do it," I said with a grin. "You like to garden, you like to visit art galleries, you like to be with your family, and you would like to have a dog. It's really quite simple."

Jan insisted that her guidance could not be so easy. Following guidance had to be much harder.

"Do you want to go to Rwanda and clean toilets?" I inquired. "Will that guidance be hard enough for you to follow?"

She nodded. She couldn't understand how having a good time could be guidance. "It's supposed to be hard," Jan insisted.

I pointed out to Jan that she had a tribal belief that following guidance meant doing something difficult or unpleasant, something that would be a sacrifice of some sort or require to her to lose something, be alone in life, or suffer in some other way. If this was Jan's idea of guidance, no wonder she'd never prayed for guidance before.

"Why would God want you to struggle, suffer, or sacrifice things?" I asked her. "That makes no sense." I explained to her, that because of our personal gifts, certain jobs are easier than others. Because of our natural inclinations, we will be drawn to various activities. Doing what you love and what is natural for you, raises your vibration.

You need to do what is right for you and in alignment with your interests and talents. Some people are meant to dig wells in third world countries, or save trees, or work long hours to clean our oceans, or volunteer their life to the support of orphaned children. The point is, *these people are not suffering in their purpose.* They love what they are doing! And that high vibration ripples out to the rest of world.

When you enjoy your life, you raise your vibration. Your happiness will be contagious. I explained to Jan that spreading joy is definitely a worthwhile purpose in life. For her this meant gardening to raise her vibration and sharing her plants and her joy. She didn't need to have a grandiose purpose to make a difference.

Then I reminded Jan of the philosophy we have at the Center for Spiritual Responsibility: heal yourself, raise your vibration, and have a positive impact upon the world. Allow your high vibration to inspire others to heal. Make a difference in the world by taking care of yourself, and thus being of service to God and others.

Jan felt between a rock and hard place. She wanted to make a difference in the world and absolutely be of service, but she was determined to make her life harder than it needed to be. She was convinced that her purpose in life could not be so easy as to simply be happy. Her purpose had to be more than that.

There was one more snag. Jan wanted her guidance to come with a step-by-step instruction book and a money-back guarantee that all would be well if she followed it. That's not always how guidance works. Sometimes you are simply given the first step. You take it, and then you have to trust.

If you have difficulty trusting what your inner voice is telling you, remember that each and every time you have followed your guidance in the past, you came out ten times better than before. Not just a little better. Ten times better, and following your guidance will lead to great things.

Steps to build your self-esteem

Growing spiritually requires confidence. Follow these techniques to boost your self-esteem. Put your answers in a log entitled "Who I Really Am." Refer to it often. I cannot emphasize enough how important this is to your spiritual evolution.

- Find out who you are. Describe yourself on paper as if you were writing about a friend. Be honest and list at least five wonderful things about yourself.

- Determine what qualities you have that you can always count on. Write down why you would choose yourself as a partner on a two-week expedition across the Canadian Rockies.

- Do the same thing with a six-week assignment to work closely together in your profession. If you find a good reason to dread that six-week assignment with yourself, consider changing some behaviors.

- Identify and own the positive things your friends, co-workers, and/or family say about you. If nothing comes to mind, ask them why they like you. For example, I heard this comment repeatedly in the E.R.: "Christel, I love working with you because you know your stuff, and no matter what happens – even if we get a busload of hemophiliacs who've been hit by a train and there's no clotting factor 8 in the hospital - you remain totally calm and get the job done. We feel safe working under you."

- Pat yourself on the back for your achievements. Do you notice the good you do or only the mistakes and failures? Think of two things you did during the day that were good for you, for someone else, or for the overall vibration of the planet. Put them in your log. If nothing comes to you, then simply say a prayer for yourself and one other person.

- Respect who you are, and if you don't respect yourself, find out why. What could you do differently so you would respect yourself? Pick one part of you that you would like to change and then focus on it for two weeks. Use your log. Make the commitment, and you will be amazed at the results.

- End your day with gratitude for your gifts and talents, your health, and something that touched your life with beauty. Before falling asleep, remember three wondrous things in your day, and tell God how grateful you are for them.

- Remember, when you downplay who you are, it does not serve the highest good of anyone. Listen to *The Confidence Code* for even more techniques to find your courage and claim your self-esteem.

Rewrite those limiting beliefs, fill yourself to the brim with confidence, and enjoy yourself, which means the rest of us will enjoy you more too!

As you treat yourself more kindly, it becomes more natural to hear with more loving ears.

Living a divinely directed life

Living with divine direction doesn't mean that your life is perfect, but rather:

Divine direction means your life will work out better than you could have hoped for, that the things you truly want in your heart will often happen, that there will be a flow, an ease and a sense of "this feels right" each day.

Divine direction means that you live according to your truth, that you do the things that raise your vibration, hang out with people you love, and feel passion and excitement about your life.

Divine direction means that you ask God to show you what you are meant to do with your life and that you are cooperating with this venture.

Divine direction means you will find meaning in your life and a sense of purpose.

Divine direction means that even when crappy things happen, you will find an inner resilience and joy in being alive.

Divine Direction gives you the freedom and energy to be more generous with others.

When you learn to listen to your intuition and live with divine direction there are many benefits:

- You will greatly reduce or even eliminate your head chatter and mental ping-pong.

- Needed answers will be soft, quiet, gentle, clear, and simple.

- With one instruction given at a time, you are less apt to be confused or distracted.

- Once you commit to that first piece of guidance, you will receive a spiritual roadmap one step at a time.

- Fewer distractions in your life will make you more available to spend time with loved ones, pursue your passions, and be of service to others, which is healing for our planet.

- You will experience the magical synchronicity that compliments and enriches your life.

Greatness requires your participation!

Chapter Ten

CROSSING OVER

That day will come for all of us when we will let go of our body. Our essence or spirit will continue and be given the option to enter the "room." We will have a choice, as we did in life, to gravitate toward the high vibration light, or not.

You won't be left alone, but will be escorted by a spiritual helper when you die. Your escort is not a grim reaper type of being who enters your room and takes you away when he decides it's your time to go. Rather, the angel or multitude of angels who come to accompany you at death are brimming with love, reassurance, and light.

As I sat at many deathbeds, it was not unusual for people to see familiar faces or remark on the beautiful light, as their spirit prepared to leave their body.

That's because there truly is light, not darkness at the end of the tunnel. Each time I have crossed over with someone who has died, a slew of bright angels meets us on the other side. It's like coming out of a dark cave into the doorway of a room filled with the softest and most inviting light you can imagine.

Anyone who has had a near death experience knows about this "room" even though they don't get to actually enter it. Although it is infinitely big, it still feels too small to hold all the love, light, compassion, kindness, and joy that are in it.

When people cross over and see that room filled with angels, they remember who they really are: a part of God. All illusions fall away and all earthly matters become unimportant as they stand in wondrous awe.

I am not allowed to enter this room. I can only stand at the threshold and look in. Frankly, I'm not sure my human brain could handle and process the magnificence on the other side. I get just a glimpse, a hint, a taste – something I experience with all my senses – before being sent back.

One minute I am with the person who has died and the next they have gone into the room and I am standing alone. The light begins to recede, and I feel like I am being sucked backward to earth.

I always return with the paradoxical feeling of being happy the person has died, because I have seen the joyful place where he has gone. Later, as my impressions of that wondrous room begin to dim, I am awash in sadness over losing them.

I know that when people die their new lives are so filled with this unconditional love, that it heals their pain of leaving us behind. Can you imagine tasting that unconditional love here on earth? You can. All of us can. This book has shown you how. Start with praying gratitude, then open your heart and ask for guidance.

I feel so privileged to even briefly get to see the ethereal bliss we experience at death. To say it is "life-changing" is an understatement. "Extraordinary" doesn't come close. Experiencing my spirit unfettered by my body is so uplifting and so ecstatic, I find it almost painful to return.

My experiences in the E.R. have shown me that no one is alone when they die. When death is imminent, an angel hovers in your room. I've seen both clusters of angels and a solitary angel waiting to accompany someone. (More angels are not better than one angel; the number of angels does not change the amount of comfort or peace you feel.)

Sometimes the light from these angels is very soft and other times extremely bright. I believe the amount of light around someone who is about to die is directly proportional to the person's need.

In the bedrooms and hospital rooms of people who have accepted their impending death, are at peace, and are ready to embrace God, I have seen one angel hovering quietly in the corner.

When people have died traumatically or suddenly there is usually a multitude of angels crowding around them. The brightest light of all is with the people who fear death and fight it to the bitter end; I think all that light reassures them and helps them on their journey to the room. People who are scared to die need a lot of light, and many angels. People who trust in the afterlife do not.

Yet even with angels lighting your way, you still have choices when you die. It is always your choice whether or not to enter that room. Sometimes people linger outside it for a day – or for years, cultivating their own agenda.

Pride can even hurt you in the afterlife, if you tenaciously cling to the need to be right (*I am unworthy and don't deserve forgiveness*) or the desire for vengeance and retribution. These lost souls need all our prayers and good intentions to find their way back to the light, and choose to step over the threshold into that beautiful and loving room.

I took my friend Teri to the threshold of the afterlife to show her what awaited her. She was dying of breast cancer that had spread to her liver, bones, and brain. When I entered her hospital room, there were angels sitting with her. It's hard to explain how comforted I felt, even though my dear friend was dying.

Although Teri could feel the angels' presence, she like most people didn't want to leave this earth. Part of her was thinking about her family and friends, and a small part of her was worried about the afterlife. She believed in God and the afterlife, but she was also a little scared that maybe it was all a hoax made up to make us feel better.

I took her hand and quietly brought her spirit to the place between heaven and earth where angels reside as they watch over us. Immediately her pain-induced agitation lessened. Her breathing slowed and became even. A beatific look spread over her face. Her jerking seizure movements stilled as she drank in the light and love of those angels.

It is impossible to be in that place and maintain our earthly qualities, like fear. The joy is immense, almost too much for our hearts to capture. Each time I go there, I don't want to return to earth. It is light while earth is darkness. It is joy rather than pain, love rather than hate, and a feeling of connection with so many other lives rather than isolation. It is the ultimate feeling of belonging.

Taking someone you love to the afterlife is both devastating and wonderful. My earthly self is sad but my divine self is ecstatic. Having sure knowledge of the beauty of the afterlife kept me sane when patients in the E.R., especially children, didn't make it and when my friend Teri died.

There were many times my earthly self wanted to protest the seeming injustice of a life taken too early. But for the person who dies, it's not that way. Their firsthand knowledge of the existence of God and that room full of angels erases all their memories of the pain, betrayal, and loss they suffered here on earth.

Teri's face after her preview of the afterlife silenced my protests to God about the injustice of her early death. She looked at me with such love. "Thank you, from the bottom of my heart," she whispered. Even though she was ghastly ill, a light emanated from her that gave us both peace. When I left her, she was serene.

Before I learned how to cross over with people, I had two glimpses of what awaits us after our death. The first was when my grandmother died, and the second was in the E.R.

I was a proud new RN when my grandmother contracted terminal cancer. The illness brought her intense pain, wasted away her body, and eventually caused her to pray for a quick death. My grandmother endured her suffering bravely.

She taught me that there is a hero in each of us, even when we feel afraid. To the end, she kept her sense of humor. At times she even became the comforter, not the one comforted. I prayed daily for her easy passage.

I had stayed with my grandmother that night because I felt she was going to die, and I had the absurd notion that she might die alone. Sitting at her bedside, I watched the release of her spirit as she drifted into a coma, ready to leave. I prayed for an angel to come to her when she passed.

Suddenly my grandmother sat bolt upright, eyes wide and gazing directly into mine. My breath caught in my throat as the light in her eyes illuminated the room, my soul, and my heart. I felt joy unlike any other, and I wept tears of gratitude for the ecstasy she was clearly feeling.

When the light in her eyes slowly dimmed, I whispered, "I love you." I felt wrenched from something my soul needed, but there was nothing I could do. The light was receding. Slowly she collapsed in my arms, smiling, at peace, and looking years younger.

Three years later, working in the E.R., I felt like I was watching my grandmother die all over again. My patient's name was Mrs. Alston. She and my grandmother looked nothing alike, but cancer seemed to hit them the same way: the pain, the wasting body, and the desire for it to be over.

Mrs. Alston's way of handling her illness was the same, too. She shielded her family from her agony, refused painkillers so she would be lucid enough to say goodbye, and fought to hang on long enough to see her son one last time, just as my grandmother had hung on to see my uncle.

I prayed for an angel to meet Mrs. Alston at death. Her time was nearing when her son finally arrived. So much was said in the simple and devoted look that passed between them. Mrs. Alston's spirit began to release quite peacefully.

Suddenly she sat bolt upright and stared straight ahead for several seconds with a look of pure ecstasy. The light from her eyes was blinding. Then she took her last breath.

At that time, I could not yet fathom what my grandmother and Mrs. Alston had seen, but I knew I wanted to see the same thing when my time came.

I now know that I will. And so will you.

About the author
Christel Nani RN, Medical Intuitive

From the time she was eight years old, Christel has had the ability to "read" a person's energetic blueprint, which includes one's past experiences, choices, beliefs, and unconscious conflicts, providing a map of the energy system that identifies what needs healing.

A well respected spiritual teacher and clairvoyant whom Deepak Chopra calls "inspiring and compelling," she has an extensive background in emergency trauma

medicine, and understands how each illness has a specific vibration.

Working with clients around the globe, and in her retreats and seminars, her Readings are an energetic diagnosis of exactly why they became sick or stuck in life, and the Priority Task that will resolve it.

Her ability to read complete strangers and know more about them and their lives than they knew about themselves, and her on-the-spot readings in her popular seminars often result in life changing moments, electrifying the room and igniting the passion of those around her.

Christel's goal is to teach people to raise their vibration, which is healing to themselves and others, and ripple that vibration out into the world, creating the "tipping point of positivity."

For more information, please go to her website.

www.christelnani.com
info@christelnani.com

Read an Excerpt

Diary of a Medical Intuitive:
*One Woman's Eye-Opening Journey from No-Nonsense
E.R. Nurse to Open-Hearted Healer and Visionary*

Shortly after I started working in the E.R., a young teenager came in feeling unwell...The doctor examined him and didn't see anything wrong.

"You're probably just working out too much," he told the young man. "But let's be sure. We'll draw some blood and do a urine sample."

I gave the boy a few minutes alone, then went back and took the little cup he handed me. As I left the examining room, I looked down and saw that his urine had a green hue. I hurried to the doctor and showed him the urine sample. He looked at me with a slight frown.

"It's so awful he has leukemia," I said with compassion. I assumed the doctor, too, had seen what struck me as an unmistakable sign of the disease.

The doctor, however, had seen nothing of the sort. He thought I was nuts – until the lab results came back showing the markers for leukemia. Then he thought I was scary.

Although this kind of sudden "knowing" happened more and more in my work as a nurse, it didn't put a dent in my obstinate denial that I was an intuitive. After all, there was no such thing.

The more I doubted the veracity of my gift, however, the stronger the evidence for it became. No matter how hard I worked at ignoring or finding logical explanations for what I was experiencing, one thing became perfectly clear. Before the lab tests were run, I knew my patient's diagnosis....

Read an Excerpt

Sacred Choices:
Thinking Outside the Tribe to Heal Your Spirit

Have you ever wondered why you work so hard, grief is so hard to overcome, or just when things start to go so well, something bad happens? I may have your answer.

Your ancestors taught you how to work, how to grieve, and why bad things happen. You have taken for granted that in their desire to protect you, they prepared you adequately for life by teaching you the way of the tribe, what they valued and what they believed to be true.

These tribal beliefs are the inherited ideas about the way life works, passed down to you from anyone who had power or authority over you as a child, which is pretty much any one who was taller than you were.

Some of these beliefs cause you to make choices that make your life harder than it needs to be, creating conflicts and inner turmoil often marked by repetitive themes and patterns. For example:

- When you are making a decision, do you feel torn between what you are supposed to do and what you would like to do?

- Do you have dreams that excite you, but find yourself exhaling in defeat as your thoughts proclaim, "That's not realistic, I can't do that?"

- Does it trouble you that some of the things you do conflict with your intuition or inner knowing?

- In general, do you feel stuck or frustrated with the way things are? These are not unsolvable conundrums. They are the result of limiting tribal beliefs. A limiting tribal belief is any tribal belief that holds you back from your best life.

The good news is that they can quickly and easily be changed once you know the steps to follow.

In this book, I'll walk you through those steps so that you can experience the health and happiness of a life in tune with who you really are and what you really want. At first, you aren't even aware that you are making choices at all…

Intentions and prayers for you

I've included some intentions, prayers, and words of wisdom to help you on your journey toward living a divinely inspired life.

Choose one prayer each week and make it your focus to move toward a higher vibration and acceptance of your innate abilities.

Please remember to direct your prayers and intentions to God, Higher Power, or a light source of high vibration and love.

Courage

Help me to focus on, and make something else more important than my fear, and take the first step I know I need to take.

Flexibility

I am willing to consider letting go of any rigid beliefs that stop me from loving myself. Teach me to see the color between what appears to be either "black or white."

Gratitude

I am grateful for my talents, my intuition, and my ability to make choices that will improve my life. Being grateful raises my vibration and brings me closer to God.

Guidance

Today I will ask for guidance from my Higher Power or God whenever I need to, and as often I need to, not just when there is a large rut in my road of life.

Help

I want to find my strength that will lead me to a place of serenity. I am willing to soften my heart and feel the loving presence of my divine helpers.

Honesty

I am open to speaking authentically and communicating clearly when I ask for guidance, and I'm ready to look at any reasons I have for not wanting to learn my truth.

Humility

I am so ready to let go of my need to be right, and my illusions of self-importance that stand between my angelic helpers and me.

Integrity

I seek to be true to my spiritual nature, discern truth from illusion, and make choices that bring me closer to God.

Kindness

Today I would like to take that extra step and be kind to others. Help me to be aware of their needs and pray for them daily.

Laughter

Today I choose to smile more often, especially at myself and not take my life so seriously. Help me to see the humor in all situations.

Openness

I do not want to waste any more of my precious energy holding on to rigid "my way is the best way" thinking. I am ready to be open to new ideas that can change my life for the better.

Peace of Mind

Please help me quiet my mind of any objections or fears that stand in the way of my exploring a new way of living.

Personal Power

Guide me in stepping forward with integrity in all areas of my life and in acknowledging my innate strengths and abilities. Let me stand up for what I know is right.

Pleasure

Today I have permission to enjoy myself and take pleasure in my life, and do what's best for my spirit.

Pride

No more false humility! I know that my abilities are a gift from God, and by acknowledging my talents I am also honoring myself.

Protection

I cherish and welcome my spiritual helpers as they watch over me, help me feel safe, and shield me from resonating with any low vibration people or experiences. Their reassuring presence lifts my spirit to let go of doubt and relax in their safe-keeping.

Readiness

Please remind me to take excellent care of myself so I can be well-prepared, energized, and available to be of service to others, and heed the call of my guidance.

Safety

I like feeling safe and secure in my life. I'll remember to ask for help whenever I need it.

Self-Acceptance

I'd like to be at peace with who I am and revel in my true self. Help me be gentle and kind to myself.

Self-Esteem

Today I will not diminish or hide my abilities; please send me opportunities to share them easily with others.

Serenity

God grant me the serenity to accept the things I cannot change, the courage to change the things I can, and the wisdom to know the difference.

Spiritual Responsibility

Please help me take responsibility for what I have chosen in life by letting go of my need to be a victim and blame others. Help me make choices that improve my life, erase doubt and worry, and raise my vibration.

Strength

I will become more aware of my abilities and call upon them when I doubt my strength to move forward in life.

Trust

Please help me to be more trusting of my intuition, and to ask for a sign if I need one. Guide my heart and mind in making decisions.

Wisdom

Help me acquire wisdom by being open and willing to explore different ideas and beliefs. When Truth resonates with my soul, let me take action.

Amen.

What People are Saying

Thank you for your gift of healing and for writing a book that gives hope to spiritual seekers.
Amy D.

I just finished your book "Diary of a Medical Intuitive" and absolutely loved it!
Susan F.

You are amazing. You're not merely gifted -- you ARE the gift.
Shirley C.

Within days of Christel's workshop I felt like a boulder was lifted from me! My father and I recently had the best three hour conversation about "everything" that we've ever had. My husband says I seem much more at peace with myself.
Tara, Charlottesville, VA

You help more people than you can possibly imagine.
Carolyn, Austin TX

You are an explosion of positivity!
Francesco, Rome, Italy